EASY PIANO

SONGS FROM

A STAR IS BORN • LA LA LAND
THE GREATEST SHOWMAN

AND MORE

MOVIE MUSICALS

20 SONGS FROM 8 HIT MOVIES

ISBN 978-1-5400-4339-9

HAL•LEONARD®

Visit Hal Leonard Online at
www.halleonard.com

Contact Us:
Hal Leonard
7777 West Bluemound Road
Milwaukee, WI 53213
Email: info@halleonard.com

In Europe contact:
Hal Leonard Europe Limited
42 Wigmore Street
Marylebone, London, W1U 2RN
Email: info@halleonardeurope.com

In Australia contact:
Hal Leonard Australia Pty. Ltd.
4 Lentara Court
Cheltenham, Victoria, 3192 Australia
Email: info@halleonard.com.au

TOMORROW
from the Motion Picture ANNIE

Lyric by MARTIN CHARNIN
Music by CHARLES STROUSE

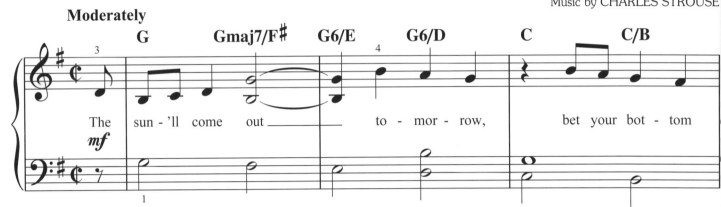

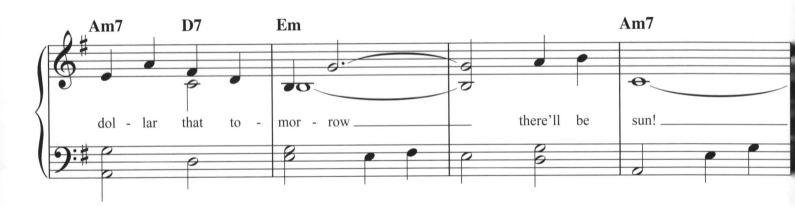

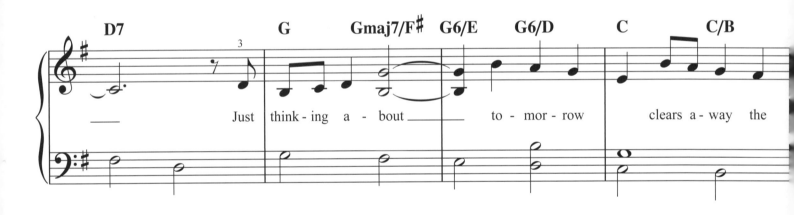

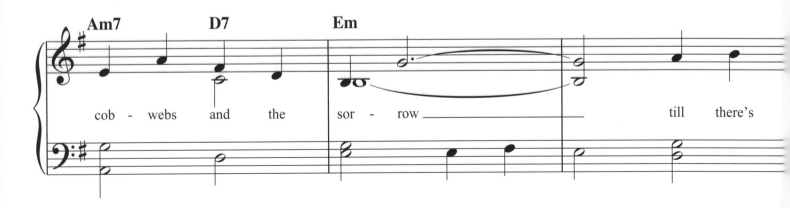

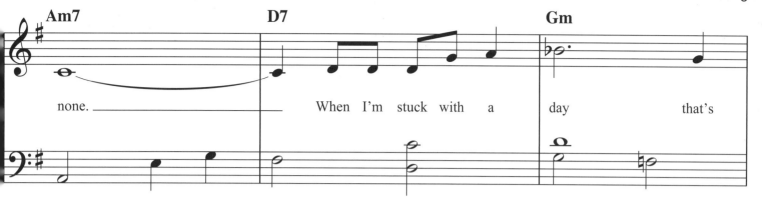

none. _____ When I'm stuck with a day that's

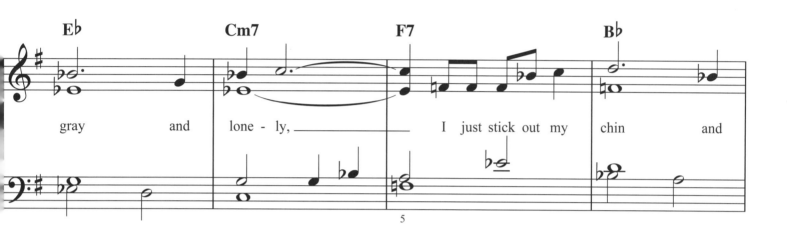

gray and lone - ly, _____ I just stick out my chin and

grin and say:

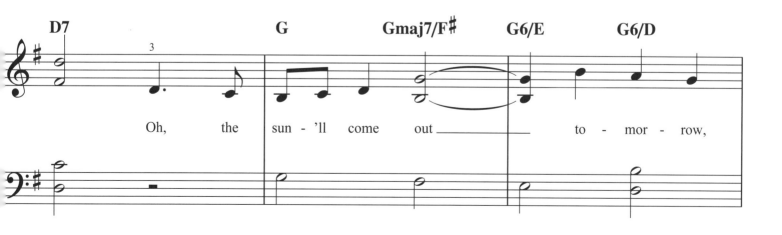

Oh, the sun - 'll come out _____ to - mor - row,

6

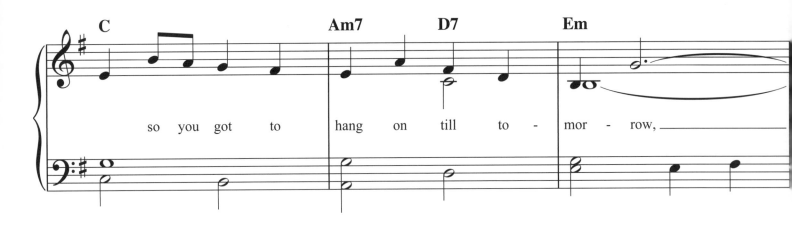

so you got to hang on till to - mor - row, ____

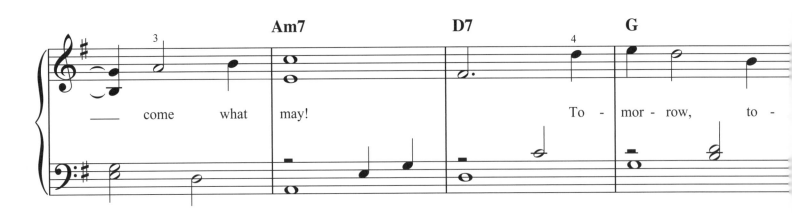

____ come what may! To - mor - row, to -

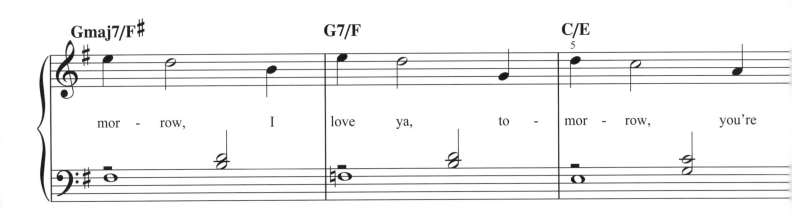

mor - row, I love ya, to - mor - row, you're

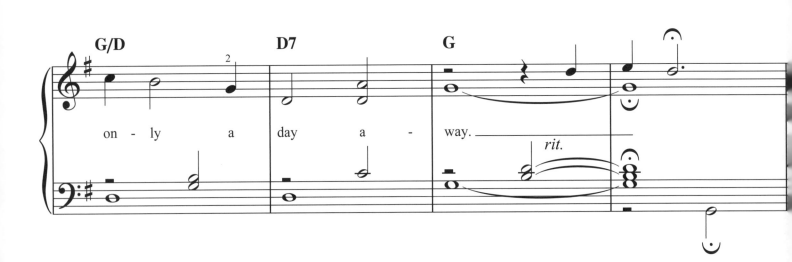

on - ly a day a - way. ____ *rit.*

EVERMORE
from BEAUTY AND THE BEAST

Music by ALAN MENKEN
Lyrics by TIM RICE

Moderately slow, with freedom

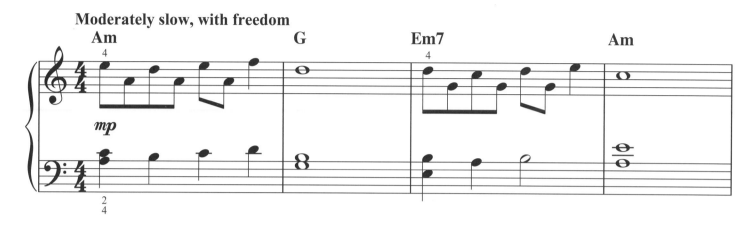

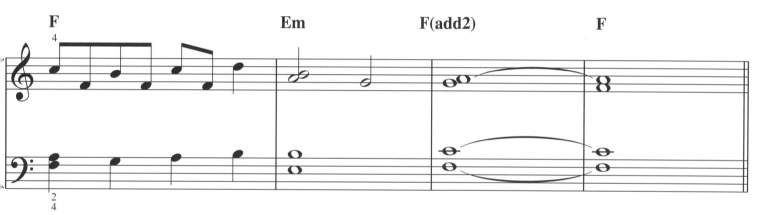

I was the one ___ who had it all;
I'll nev-er shake ___ a-way the pain.

I was the mas-ter of my
I close my eyes, ___ but she's still

fate.
there.

I nev-er need-ed an-y-bod-y in my life;
I let her steal in-to my mel-an-chol-y heart;

I learned the truth — too late.
it's more than I — can

bear. —

— Now I know she'll nev - er leave me, e - ven as she runs a-

way. She will still tor - ment — me, calm me, hurt — me, move me, come what

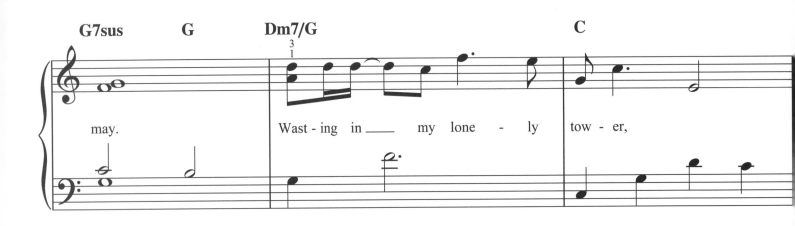

may. Wast - ing in — my lone - ly tow - er,

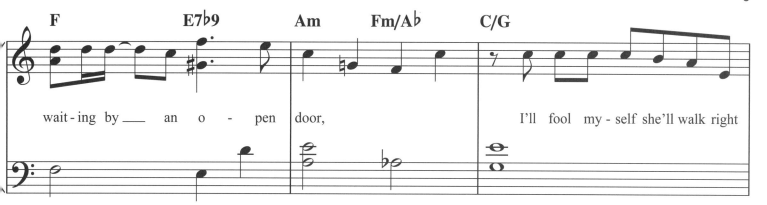

waiting by ___ an o - pen door, I'll fool my - self she'll walk right

in, and be with me for ev - er - more.

I rage a - gainst ___ the trials of love.

I curse the fad - ing of the light. Though she's al - read - y flown so

10

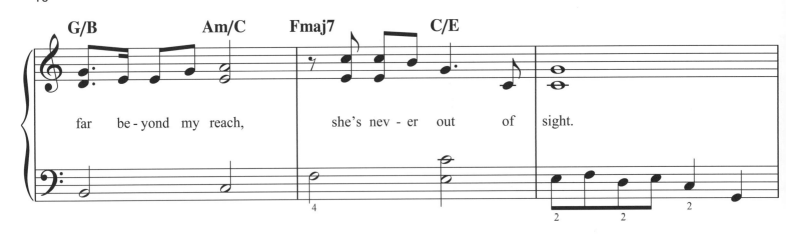

far be-yond my reach, she's nev-er out of sight.

Now I know she'll nev - er leave me, e - ven as she fades from

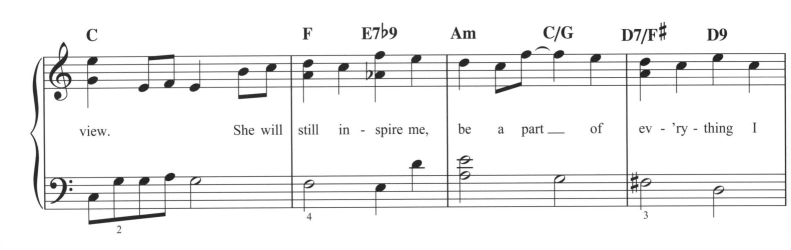

view. She will still in - spire me, be a part __ of ev - 'ry - thing I

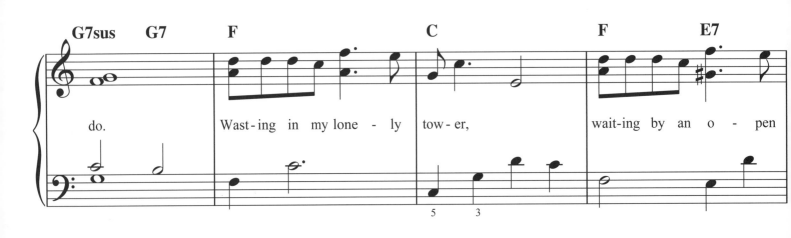

do. Wast-ing in my lone - ly tow-er, wait-ing by an o - pen

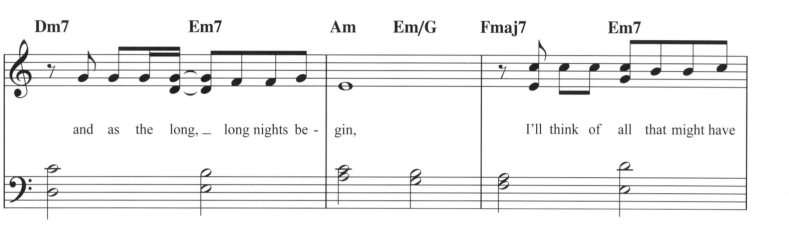

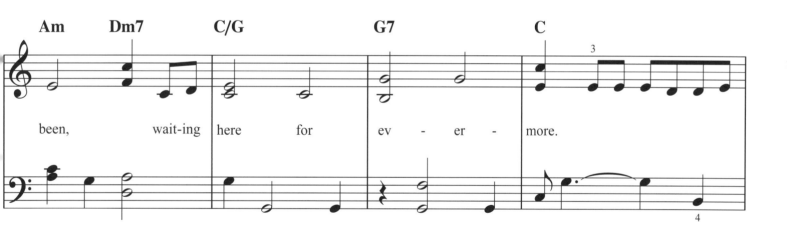

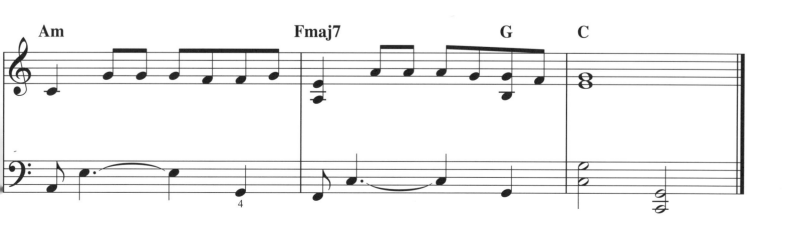

HOW DOES A MOMENT LAST FOREVER

from BEAUTY AND THE BEAST

Music by ALAN MENKEN
Lyrics by TIM RICE

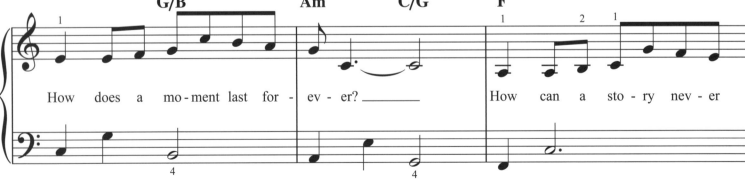

How does a mo-ment last for-ev-er? _____ How can a sto-ry nev-er

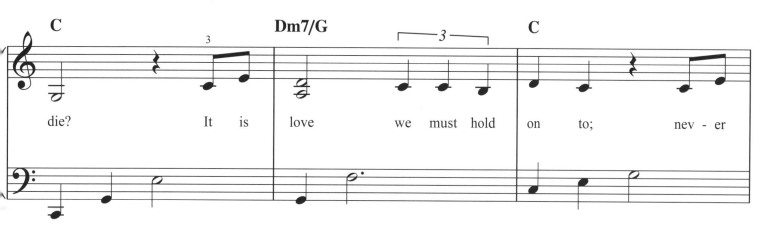

die? It is love we must hold on to; nev - er

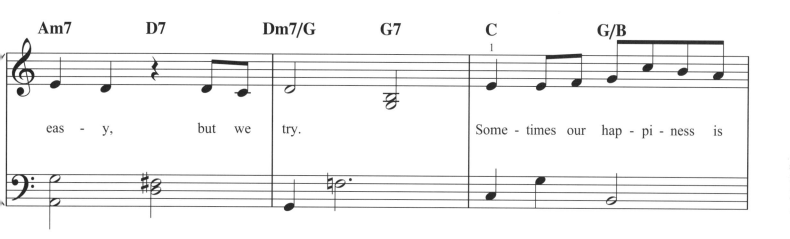

eas - y, but we try. Some - times our hap - pi - ness is

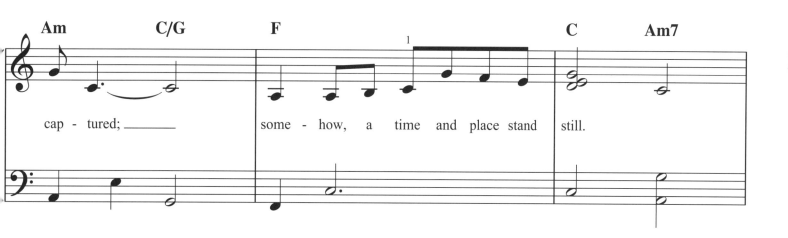

cap - tured; _____ some - how, a time and place stand still.

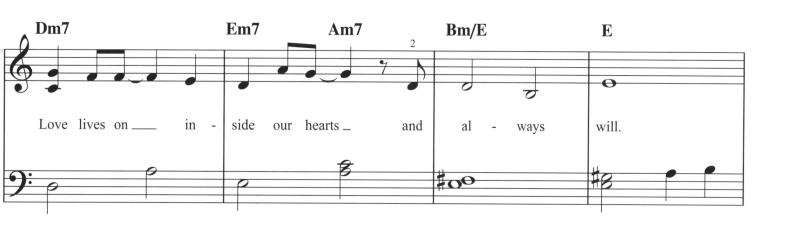

Love lives on ___ in - side our hearts _ and al - ways will.

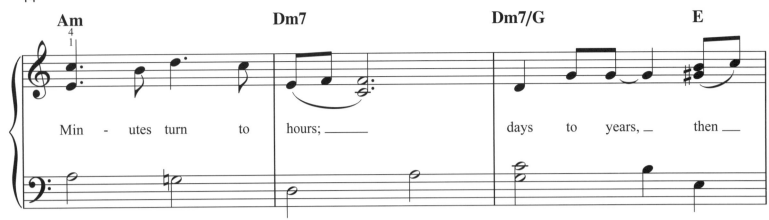

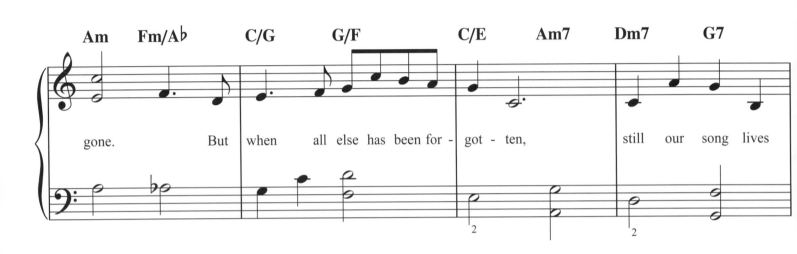

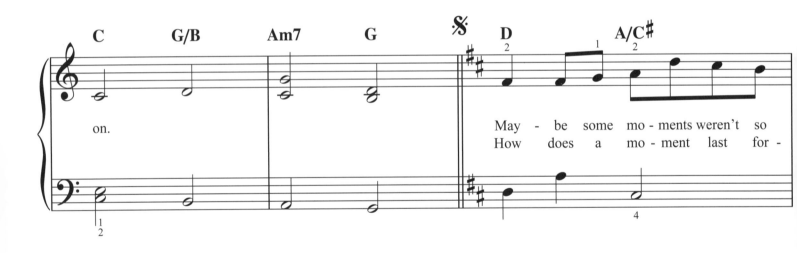

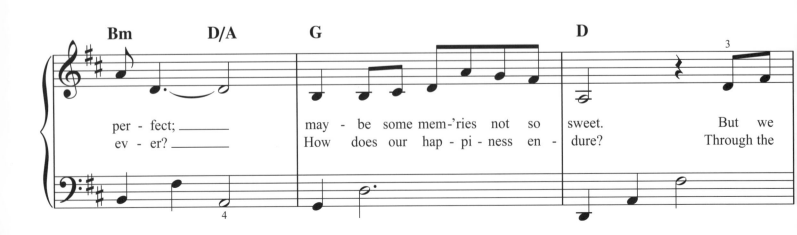

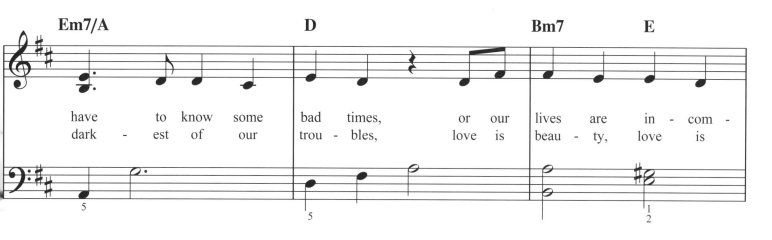

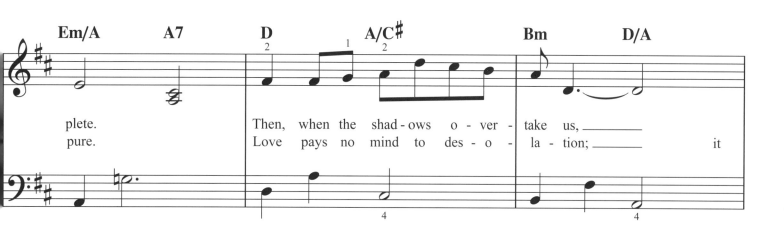

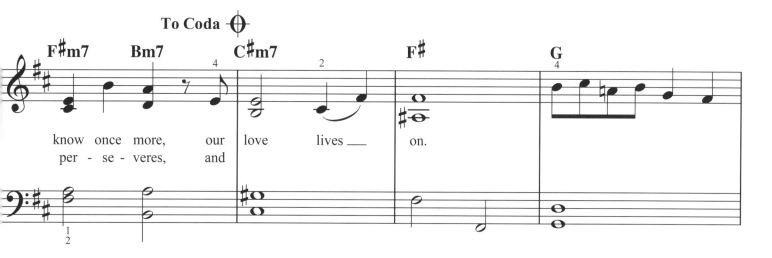

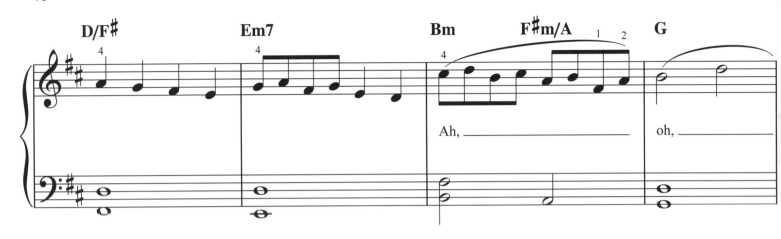

Ah, _____ oh, _____

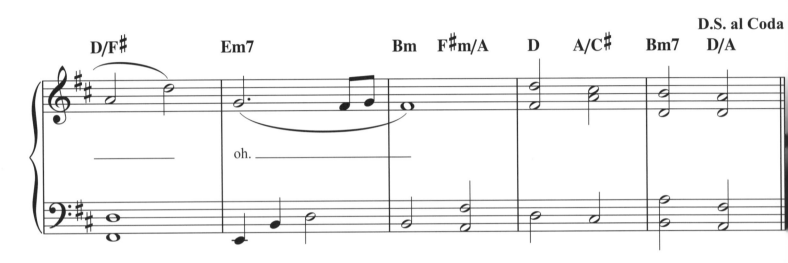

_____ oh. _____

D.S. al Coda

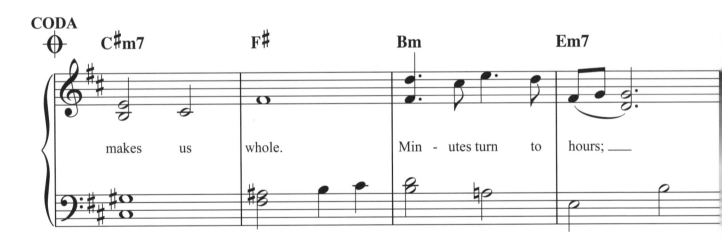

makes us whole. Min - utes turn to hours; ___

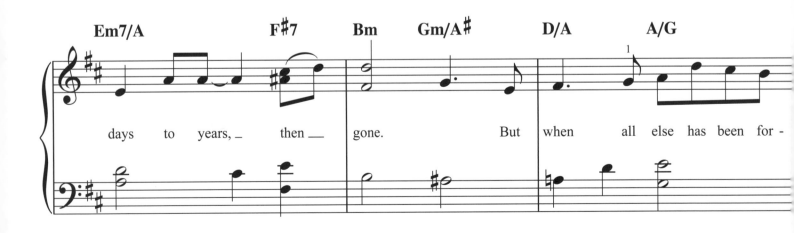

days to years, ___ then ___ gone. But when all else has been for -

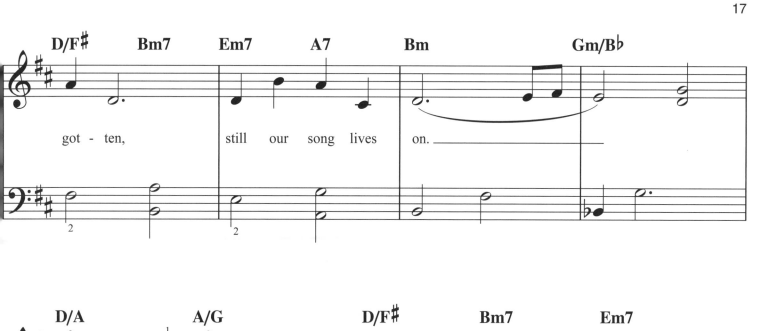

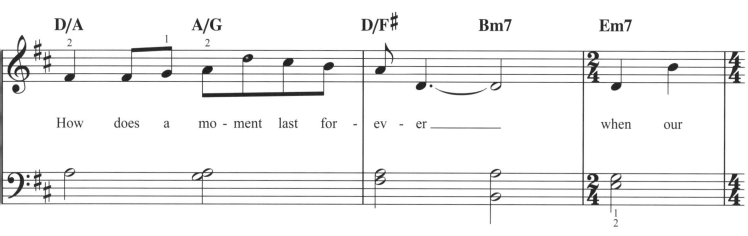

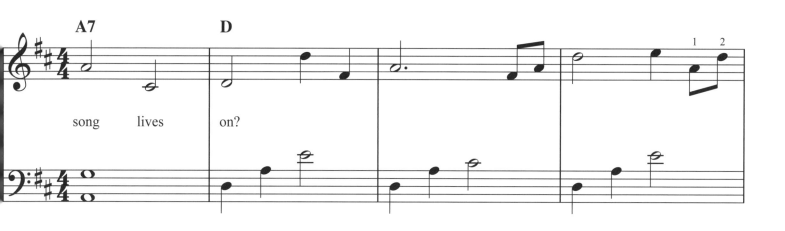

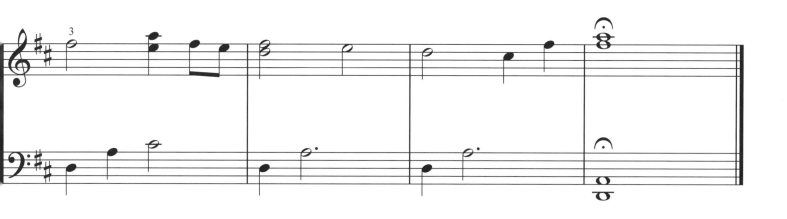

A MILLION DREAMS

from THE GREATEST SHOWMAN

Words and Music by BENJ PASEK
and JUSTIN PAUL

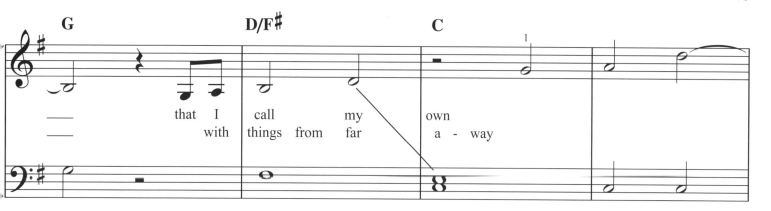

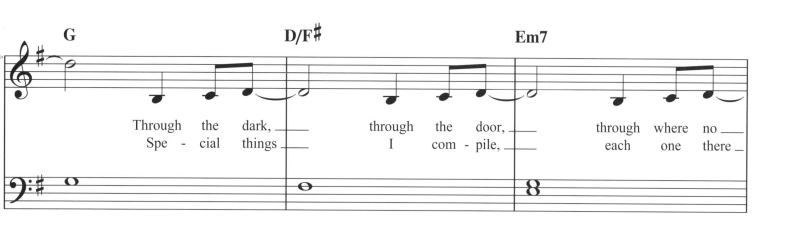

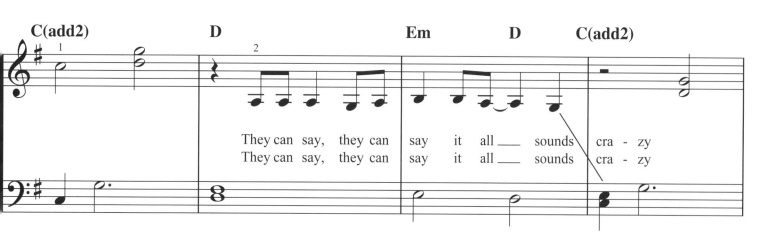

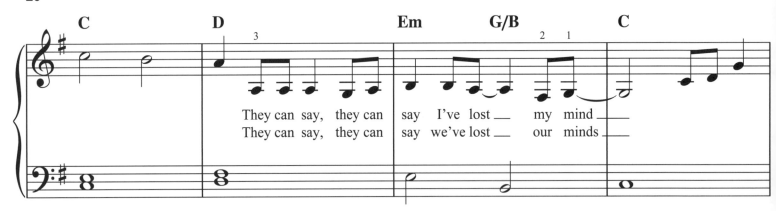

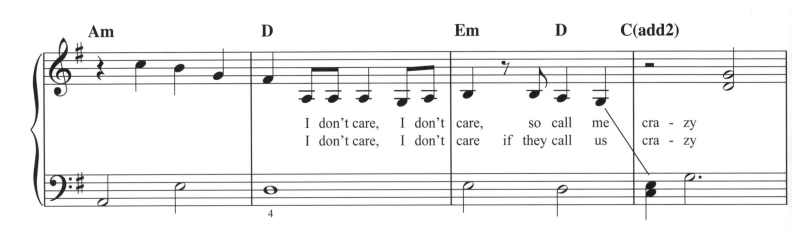

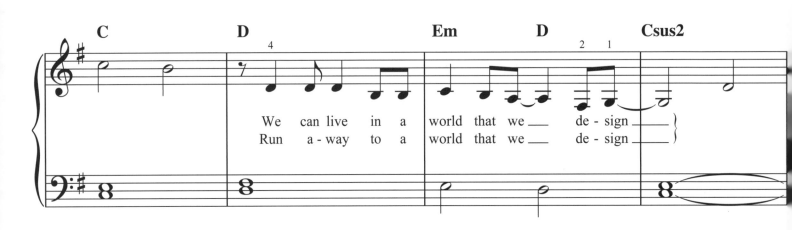

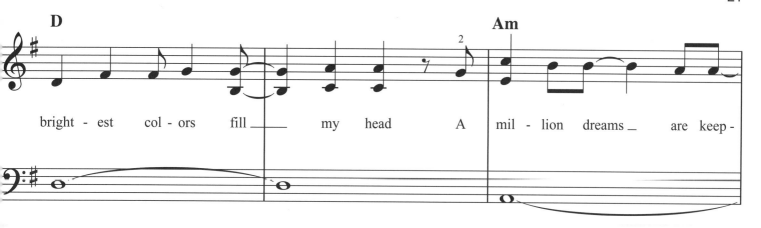

brightest colors fill my head A million dreams are keep-

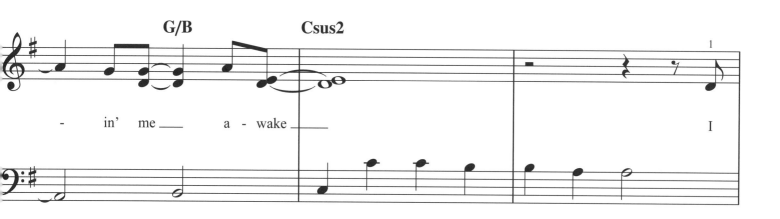

-in' me awake I

think of what the world could be, a vision of the one

I see A million dreams is all it's gonna take

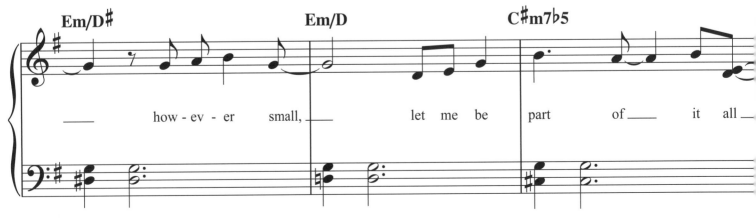

24

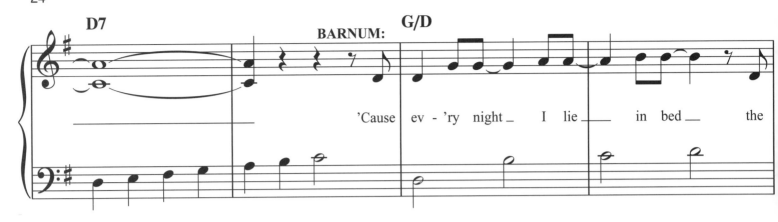

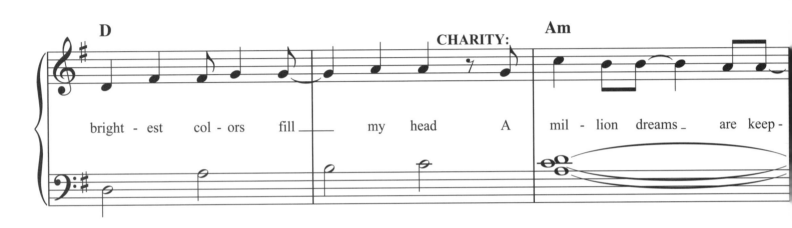

mil - lion dreams ___ is all ___ it's gon - na take ___

A mil - lion dreams ___ for the world we're gon - na make ___

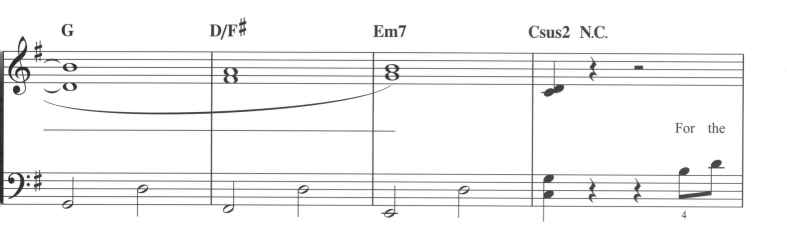

For the

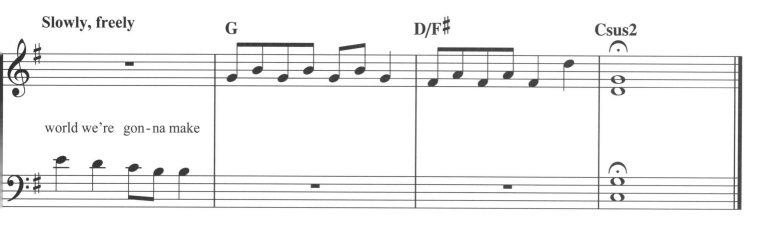

world we're gon-na make

THIS IS ME
from THE GREATEST SHOWMAN

Words and Music by BENJ PASEK
and JUSTIN PAUL

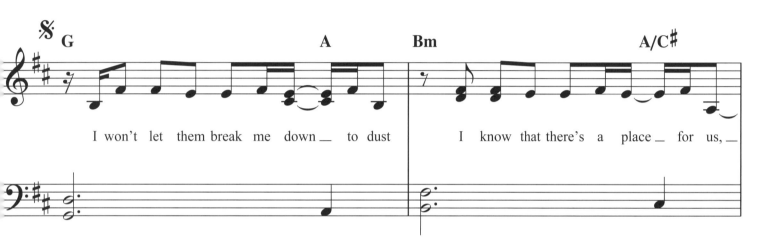

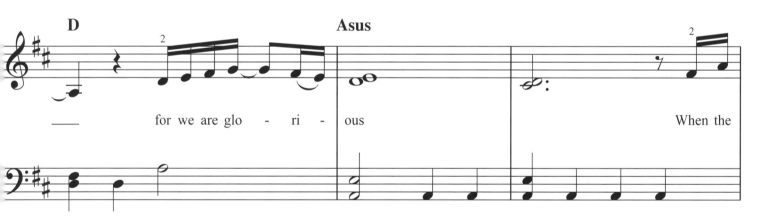

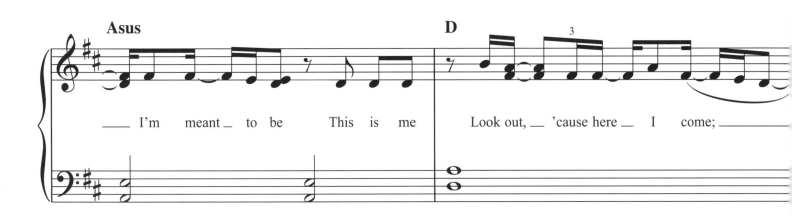

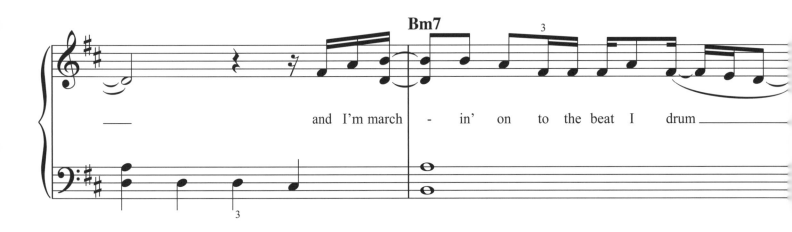

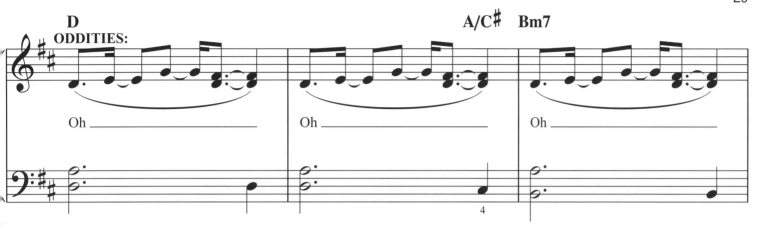

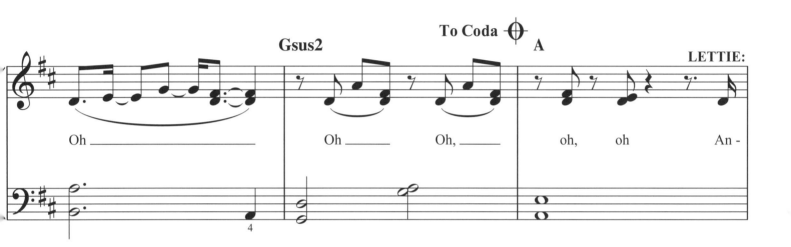

30

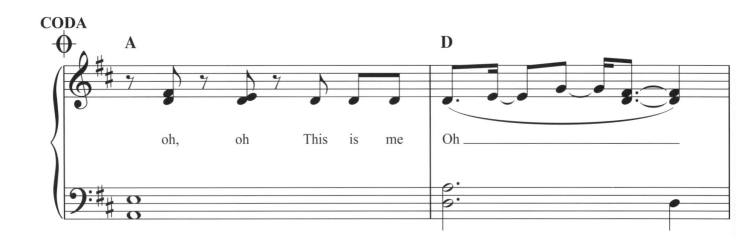

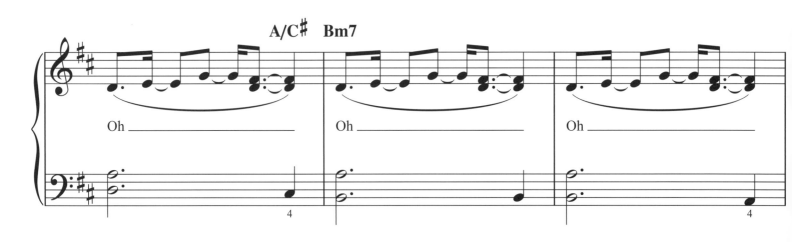

ON THE STEPS OF THE PALACE
(Film Version)
from INTO THE WOODS

Music and Lyrics by
STEPHEN SONDHEIM

32

make a de - ci - sion.
Why not
stay and be caught? Should I
mp
sim.
give that a thought, What would
be his re - sponse?
cresc.
But then
what if he knew Who I
am when I know That I'm
not what he thinks That he
p
wants?
mp
Or then
what if I am

34

know that you'll nev - er be - long? And which-

ev - er you pick, Do it quick, 'Cause you're start - ing to stick To the steps of the

pal - ace. It's my first big de - ci - sion.

The choice is - n't eas - sy to make. To ar-

rive at a ball Is ex - cit - ing and all— Once you're there, though, it's scar - y.

And it's fun to de - ceive When you know you can leave, But you

have to be war - y. There's a lot that's at stake, But I've

stalled long e - nough, 'Cause I'm still stand - ing stuck In the stuff on the steps... Bet - ter

poco cresc.

38

think-ing it through, Things don't have to col-lide—

mf brilliante

I know what my de-ci-sion is, Which is not to de-

mp

cide. I'll just leave him a clue: For ex-am-ple, a

shoe. And then see what he'll do. Now it's he and not

you Who'll be stuck with a shoe, In a stew, In the goo,
And I've learned some-thing, too, Some-thing
cresc.
I nev - er knew,
On the steps of the
mf
pal - ace!
tr
f

AUDITION
(The Fools Who Dream)
from LA LA LAND

Music by JUSTIN HURWITZ
Lyrics by BENJ PASEK & JUSTIN PAUL

Slowly and freely

Bare - foot, ___ she smiled, ___ leapt with - out

look - ing, _____ and tum - bled in - to the

In time (slowly)

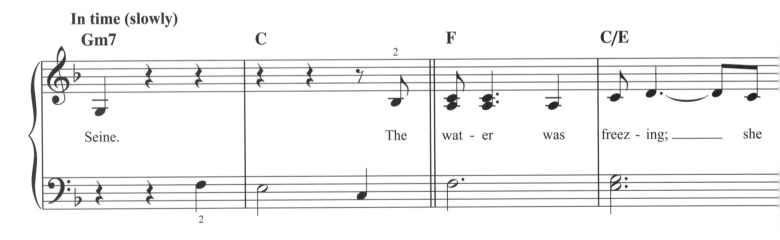

Seine. The wat - er was freez - ing; ___ she

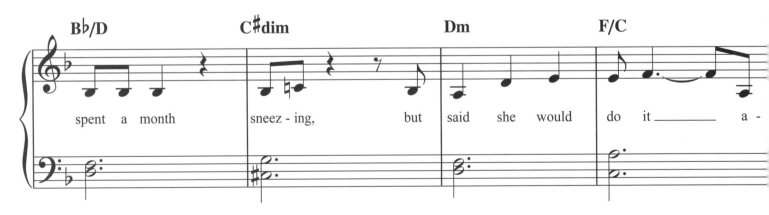

spent a month sneez - ing, but said she would do it ___ a -

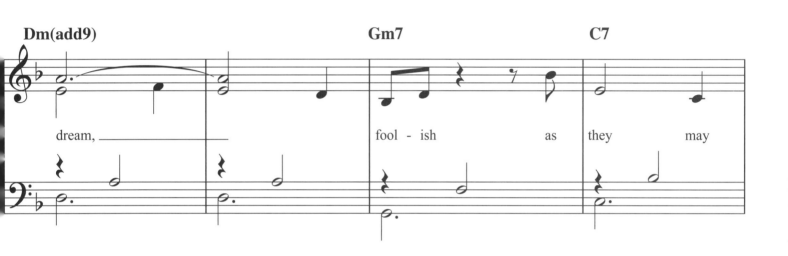

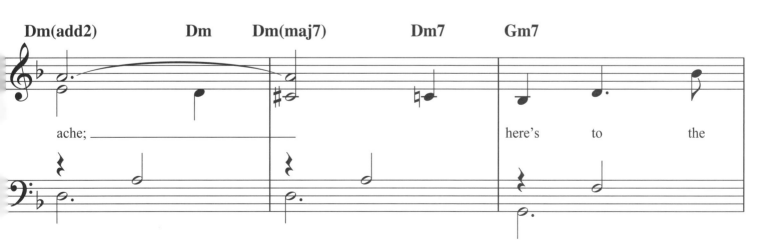

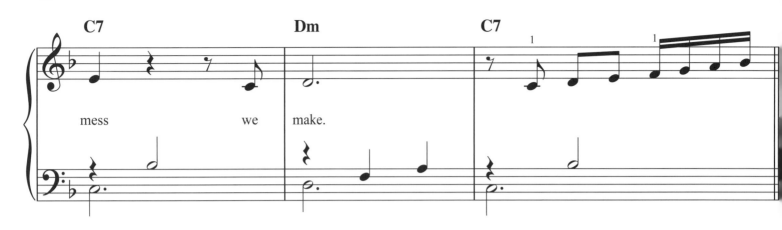

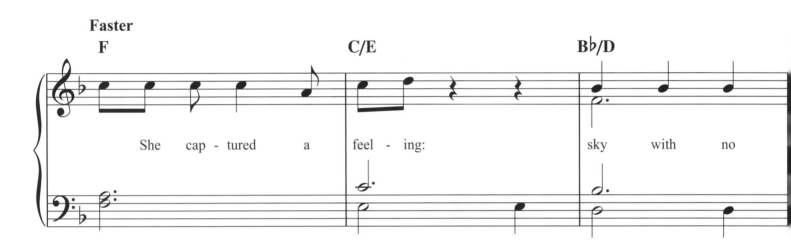

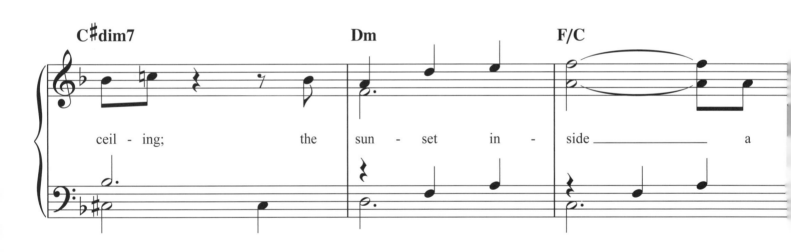

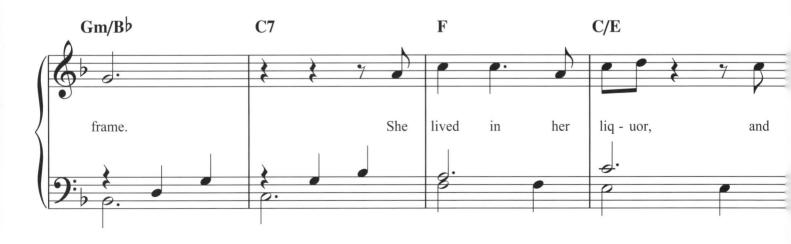

died with a flick - er; I'll al - ways re - mem - ber the

flame. Here's to the ones who

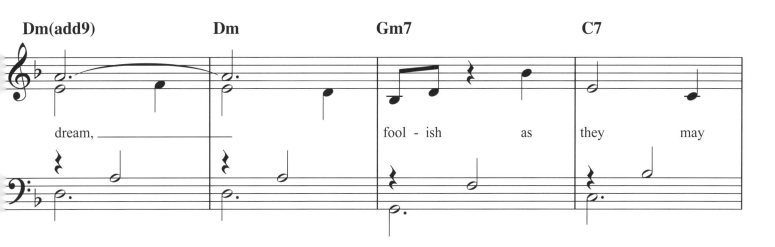

dream, _____ fool - ish as they may

seem. _____ Here's to the hearts that

44

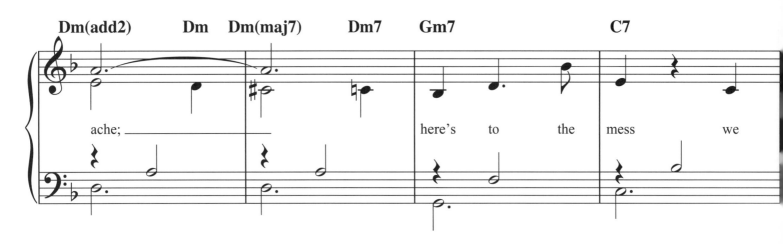

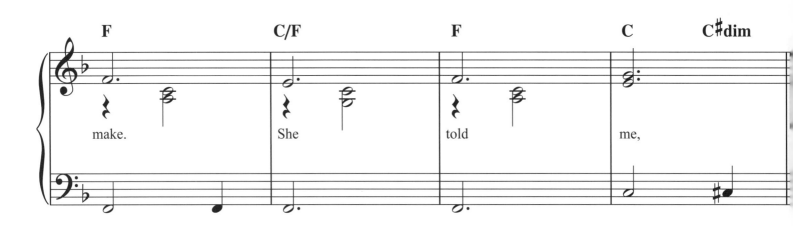

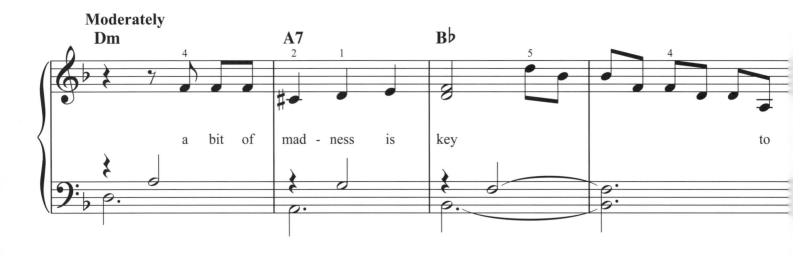

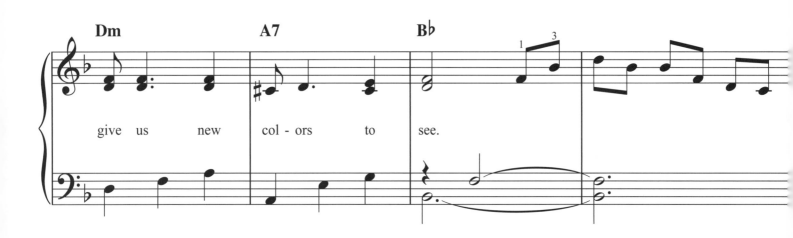

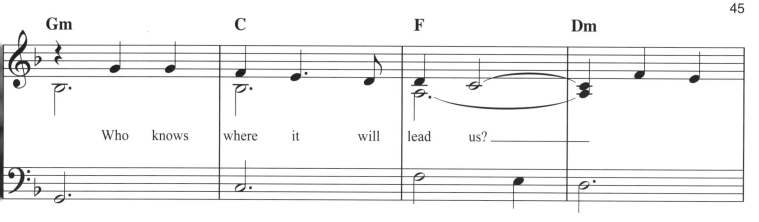

Who knows where it will lead us? ____

And that's why they need us. So,

Broadening

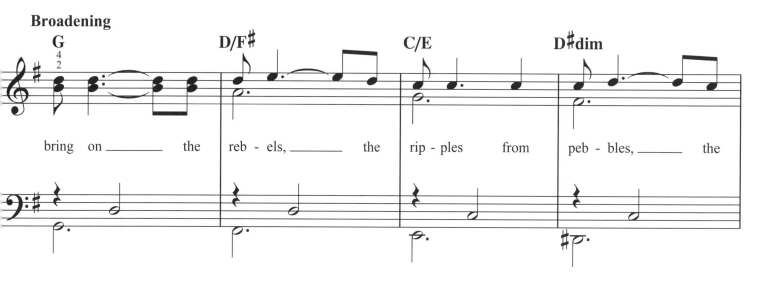

bring on ____ the reb - els, ____ the rip - ples from peb - bles, ____ the

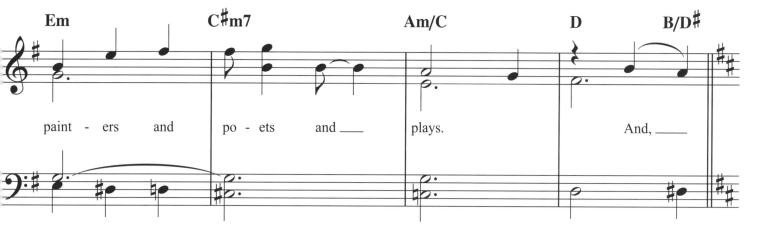

paint - ers and po - ets and ____ plays. And, ____

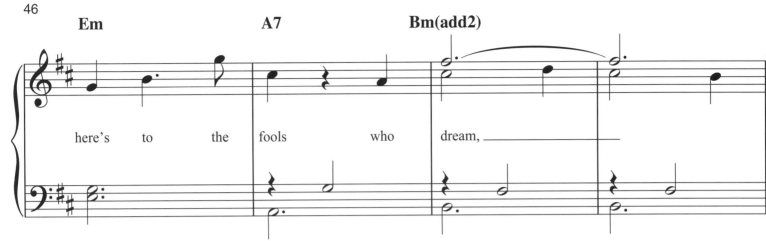

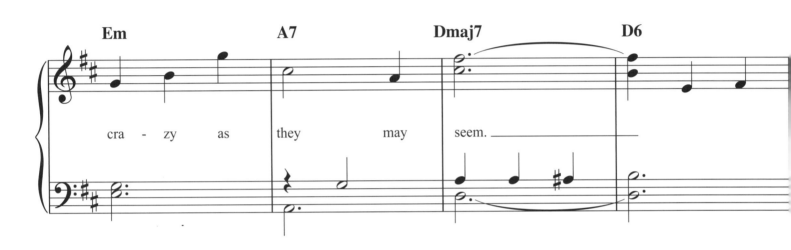

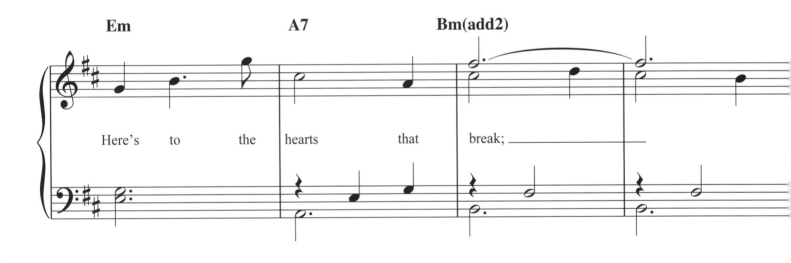

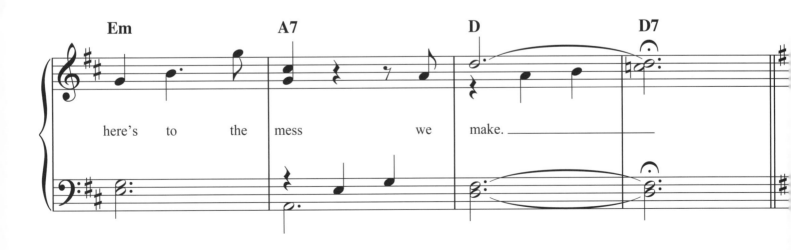

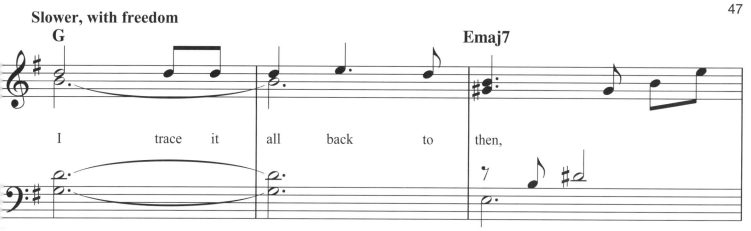

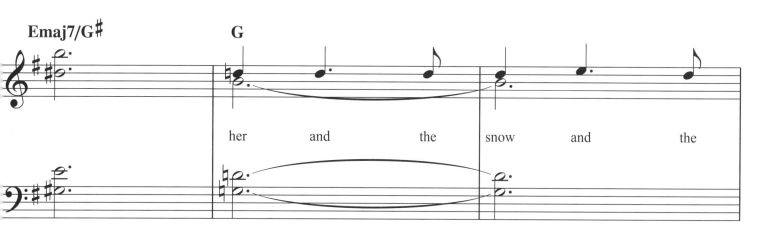

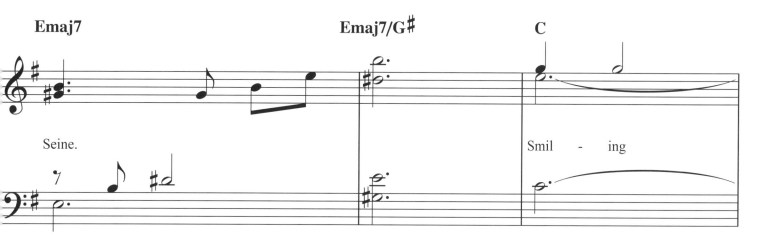

CITY OF STARS

from LA LA LAND

Music by JUSTIN HURWITZ
Lyrics by BENJ PASEK & JUSTIN PAUL

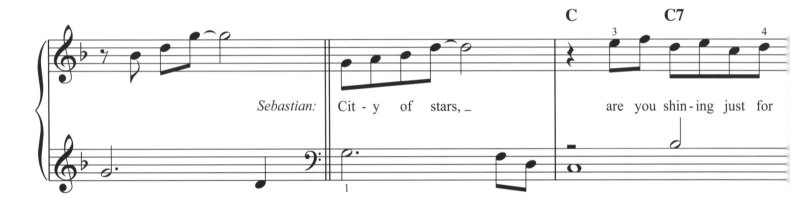

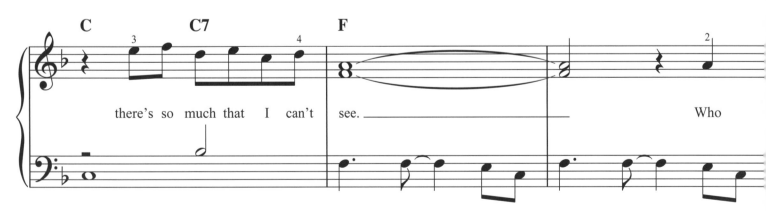

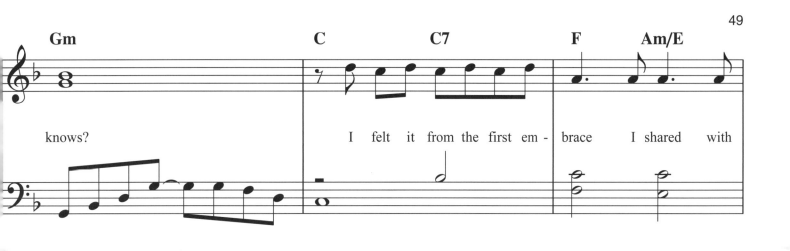

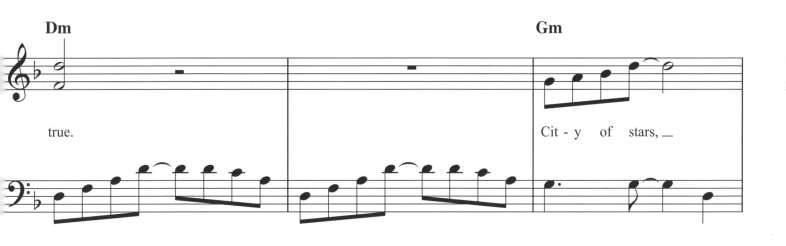

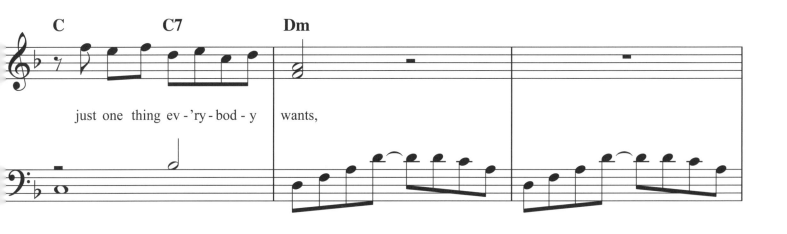

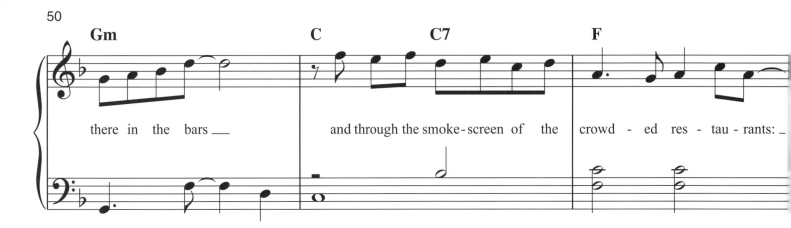

there in the bars ___ and through the smoke-screen of the crowd - ed res - tau - rants: ___

___ it's love. Yes, all we're look - ing for is

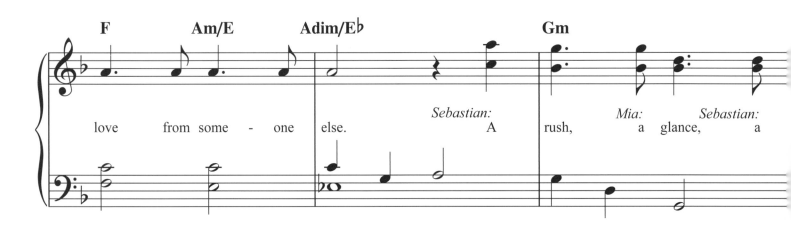

love from some - one else. *Sebastian:* A rush, *Mia:* a glance, *Sebastian:* a

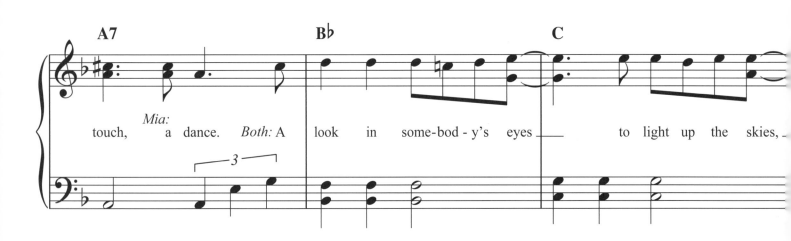

Mia: touch, a dance. *Both:* A look in some-bod - y's eyes ___ to light up the skies,

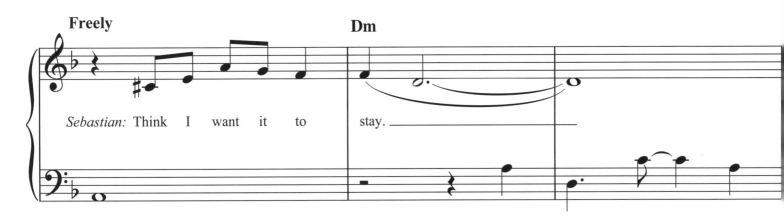

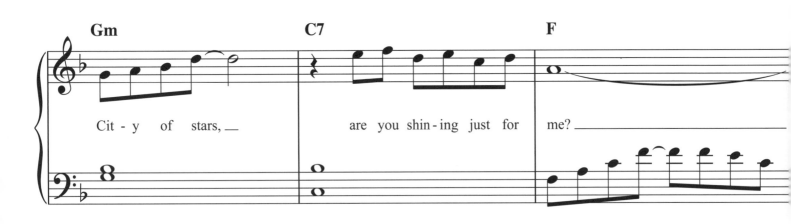

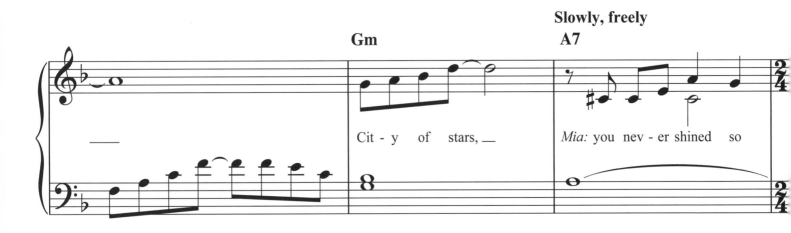

I DREAMED A DREAM
from LES MISÉRABLES

Music by CLAUDE-MICHEL SCHÖNBERG
Lyrics by ALAIN BOUBLIL,
JEAN-MARC NATEL and HERBERT KRETZMER

part,   as they turn your dream to   shame. _____

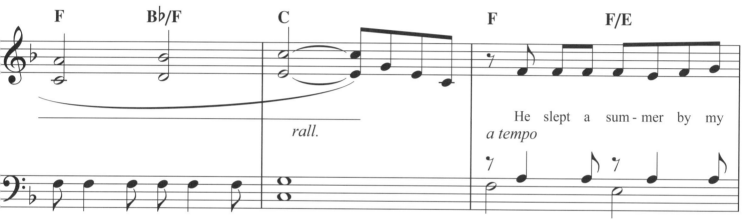

_____ _rall._   He slept a sum-mer by my

a tempo

side.   He filled my days with end-less   won - der.

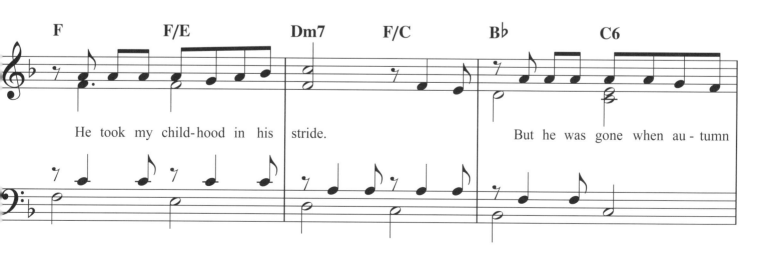

He took my child-hood in his   stride.   But he was gone when au - tumn

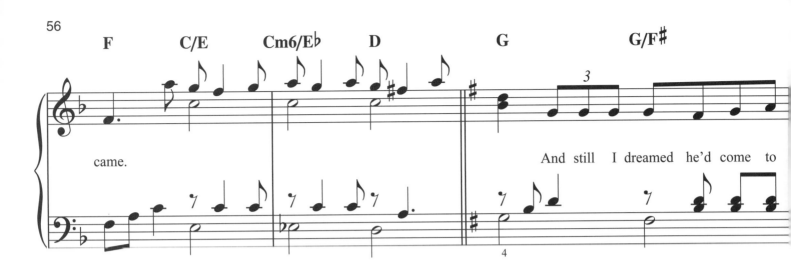

came.

And still I dreamed he'd come to

me,

that we would live the years to - geth - er.

But there are dreams that can - not

be,

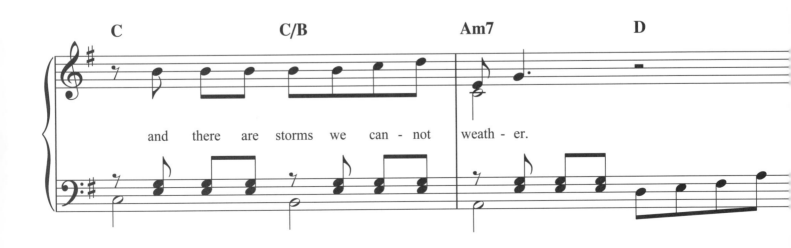

and there are storms we can - not

weath - er.

SUDDENLY
from LES MISÉRABLES

Music by CLAUDE-MICHEL SCHÖNBERG
Lyrics by HERBERT KRETZMER and ALAIN BOUBLIL

gun. Sud-den-ly the world

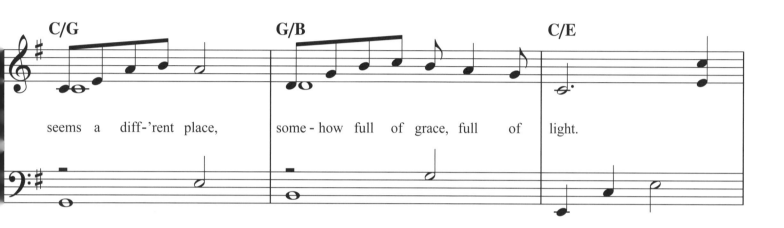

seems a diff-'rent place, some-how full of grace, full of light.

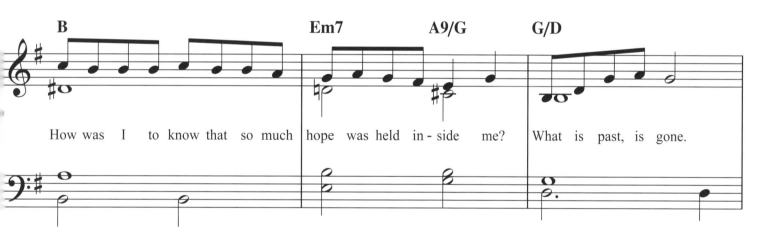

How was I to know that so much hope was held in-side me? What is past, is gone.

A little faster

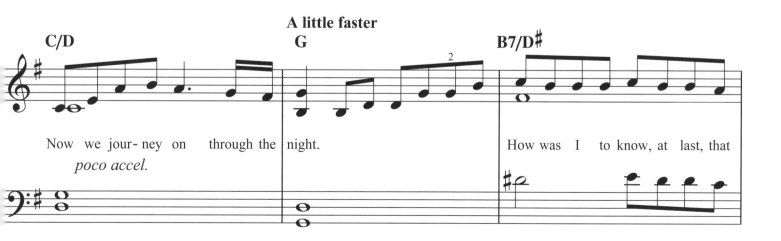

Now we jour-ney on through the night. How was I to know, at last, that

poco accel.

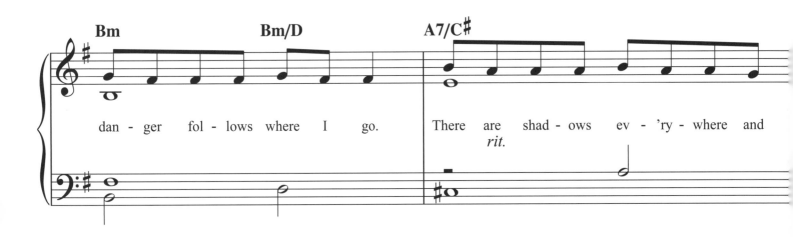

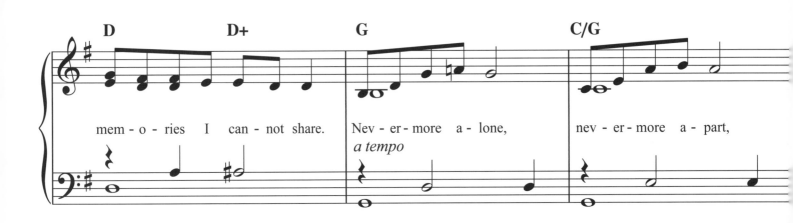

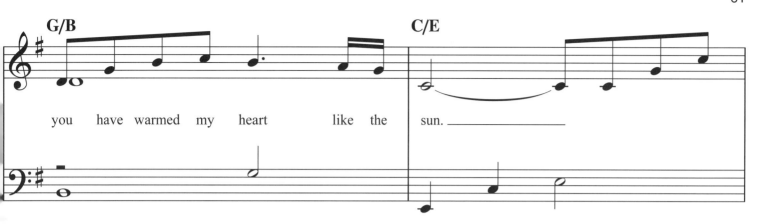

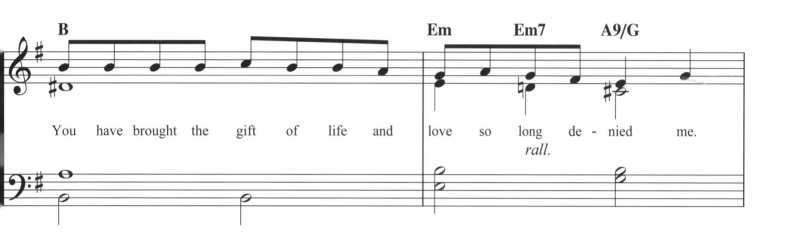

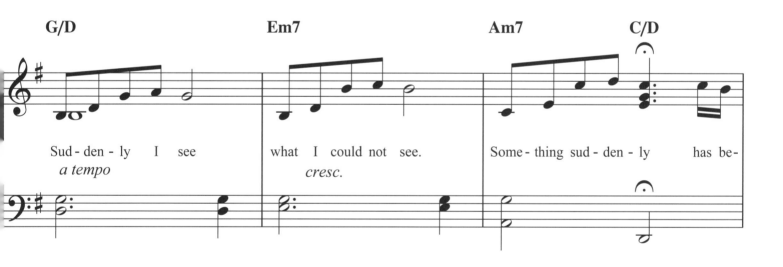

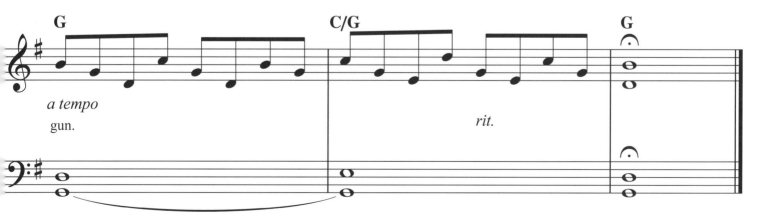

FERNANDO

from MAMMA MIA! HERE WE GO AGAIN

Words and Music by BENNY ANDERSSON,
BJÖRN ULVAEUS and STIG ANDERSON

Can you hear the drums, Fer - nan - do?
They were clos - er now, Fer - nan - do.
Now we're old and grey, Fer - nan - do.

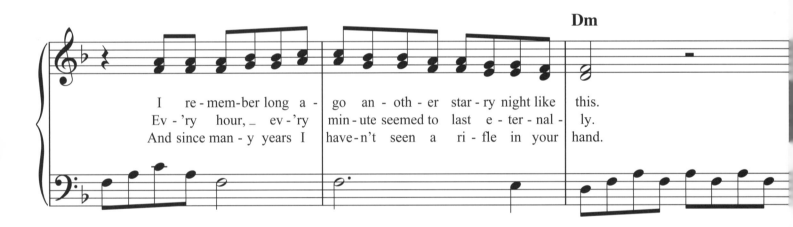

I re - mem - ber long a - go an - oth - er star - ry night like this.
Ev - 'ry hour, __ ev - 'ry min - ute seemed to last e - ter - nal - ly.
And since man - y years I have-n't seen a ri - fle in your hand.

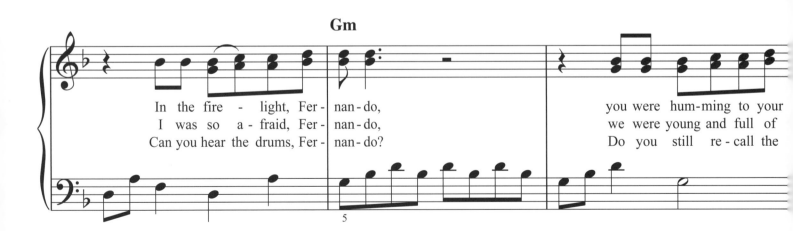

In the fire - light, Fer - nan - do, you were hum - ming to your
I was so a - fraid, Fer - nan - do, we were young and full of
Can you hear the drums, Fer - nan - do? Do you still re - call the

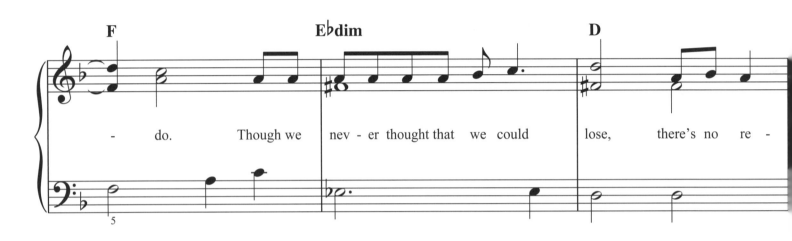

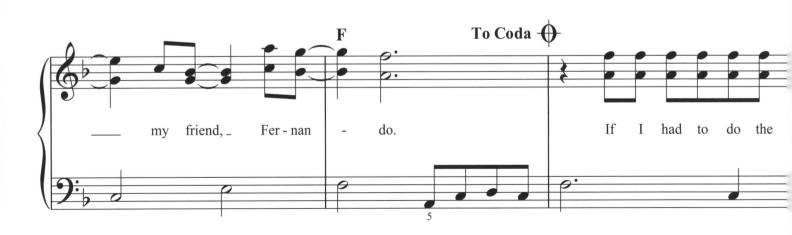

same a - gain, __ I would, ___ my friend, _ Fer - nan - do.

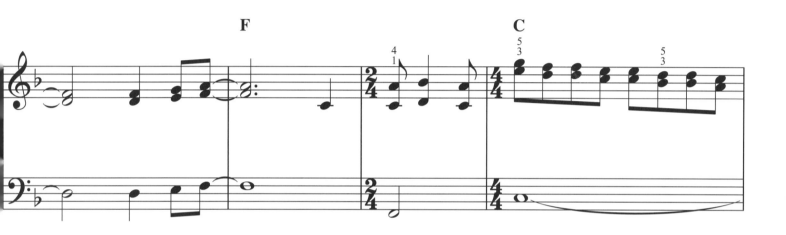

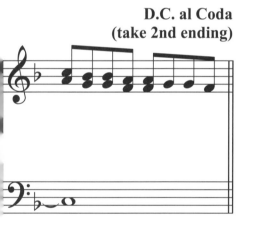

D.C. al Coda
(take 2nd ending)

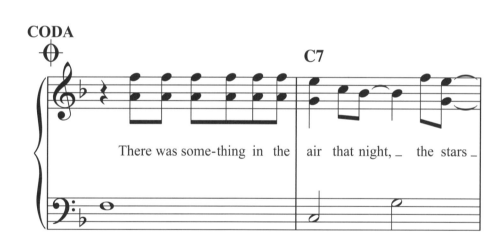

CODA

There was some-thing in the air that night, _ the stars _

__ were bright, _ Fer - nan - do.

They were shin - ing there for

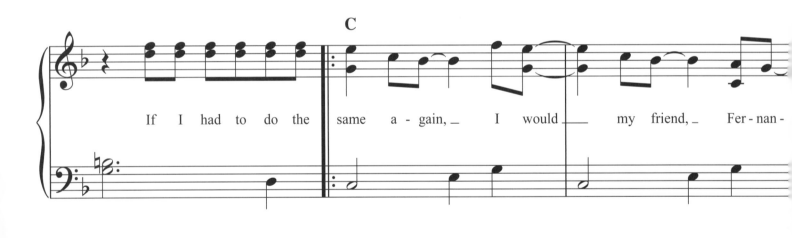

MAMMA MIA

from MAMMA MIA! HERE WE GO AGAIN

Words and Music by BENNY ANDERSSON,
BJÖRN ULVAEUS and STIG ANDERSON

I was cheat-ed by you _
I was an-gry and sad _

___ and I think you know when.
___ a - bout things that you do.

So I made up my mind ___ it must come to an
I can't count all the times ___ that I've cried o - ver

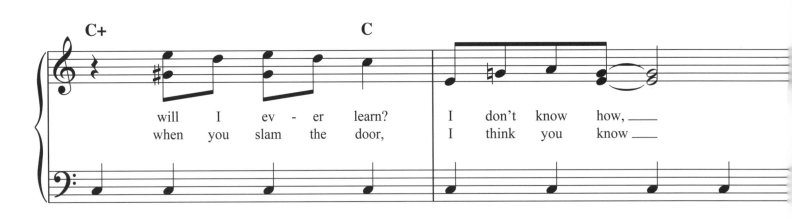

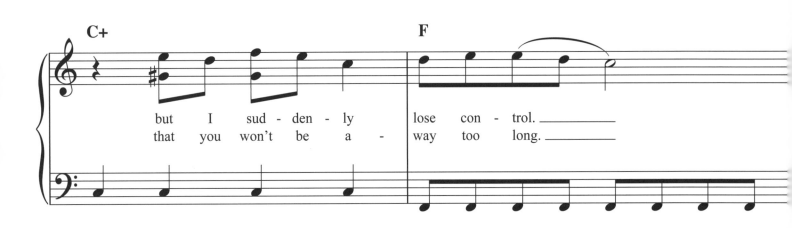

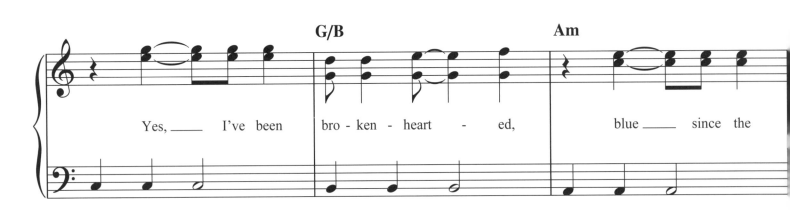

1.
Dm7   **G**   **C**   **C+**

I should not have let you go. ___

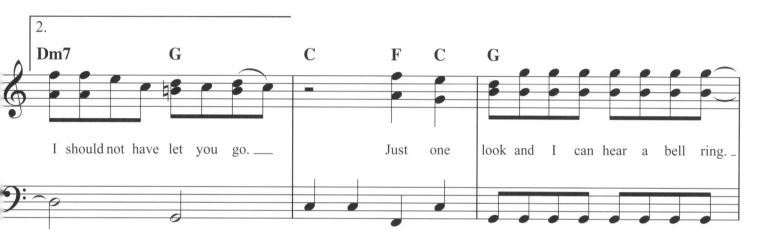

2.
Dm7   **G**   **C**   **F**   **C**   **G**

I should not have let you go. ___   Just one   look and I can hear a bell ring. __

F   **C**   **G**   **D.S. al Coda**

___   One more   look and I for - get ev - 'ry - thing, ___   oh, ___ oh. ___

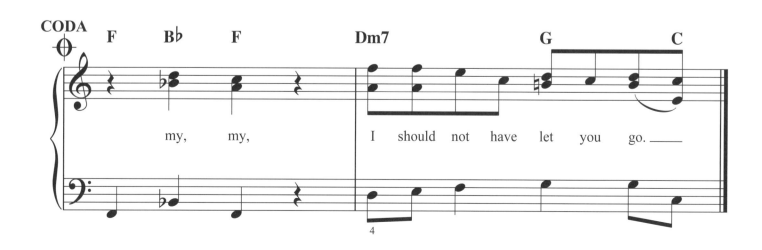

CODA   **F**   **B♭**   **F**   **Dm7**   **G**   **C**

my,   my,   I should not have let you go. ___

4

SUPER TROUPER

from MAMMA MIA! HERE WE GO AGAIN

Words and Music by BENNY ANDERSSON
and BJÖRN ULVAEUS

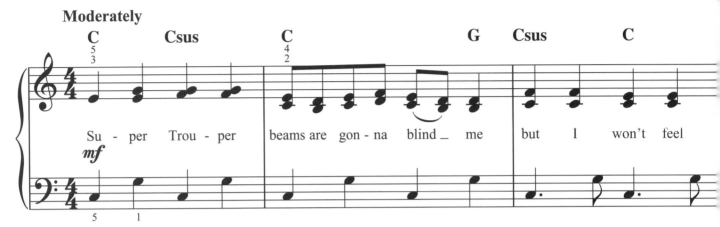

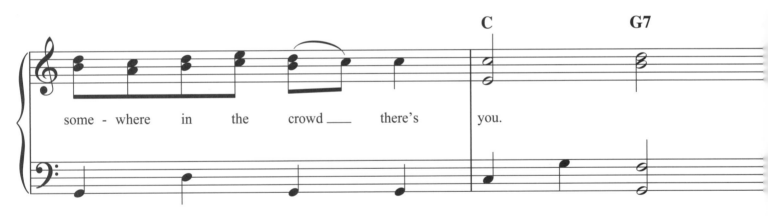

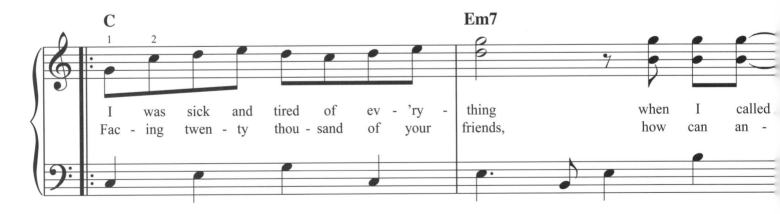

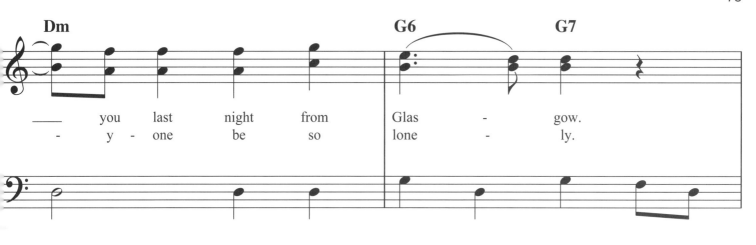

you last night from Glas - gow.
- y - one be so lone - ly.

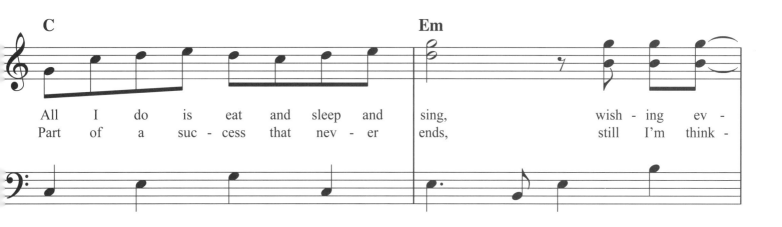

All I do is eat and sleep and sing, wish - ing ev -
Part of a suc - cess that nev - er ends, still I'm think -

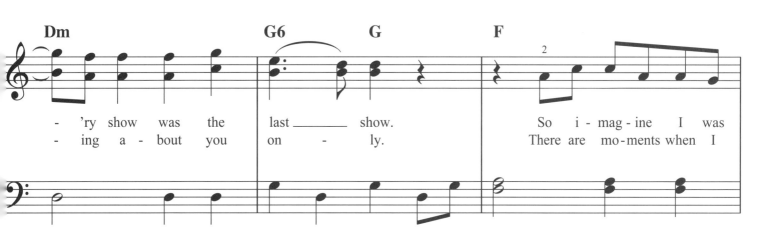

- 'ry show was the last show. So i - mag - ine I was
- ing a - bout you on - ly. There are mo - ments when I

glad to hear you're com - ing, sud - den - ly I feel al - right,
think I'm go - ing cra - zy, but it's gon - na be al - right,

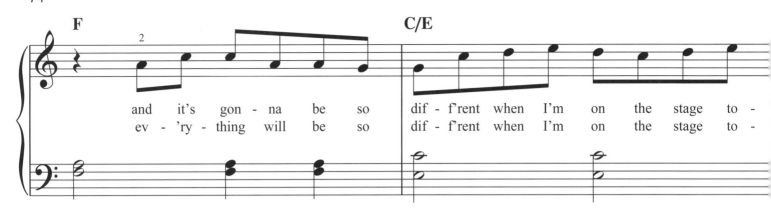

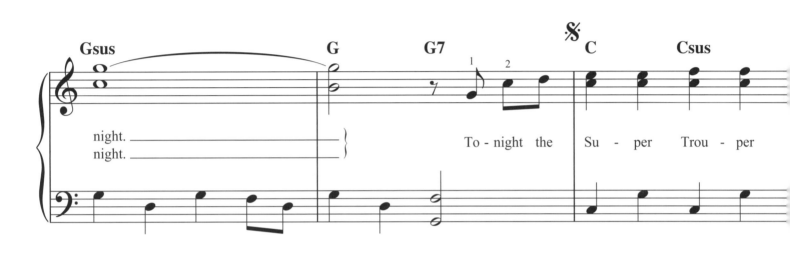

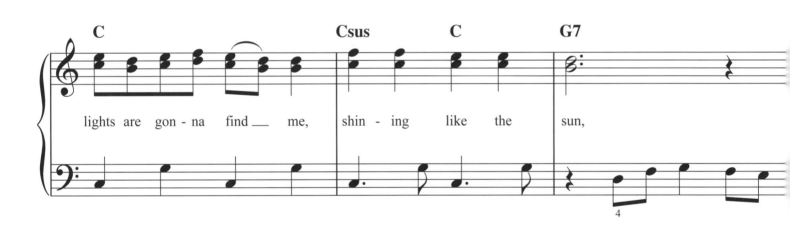

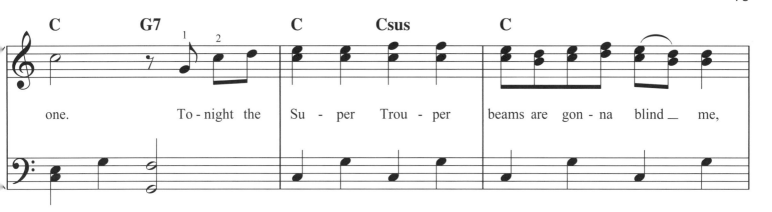

To Coda ⊕

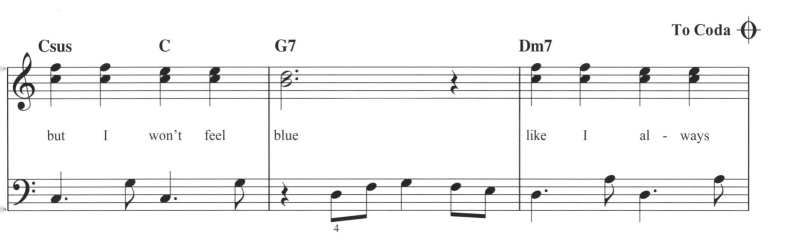

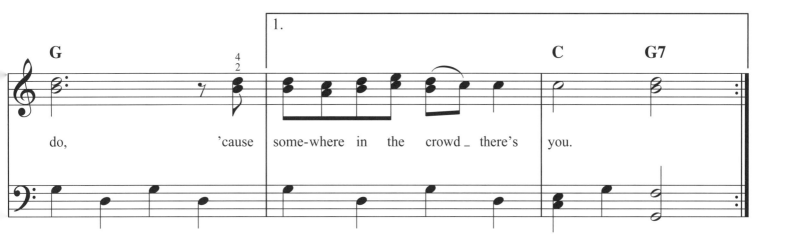

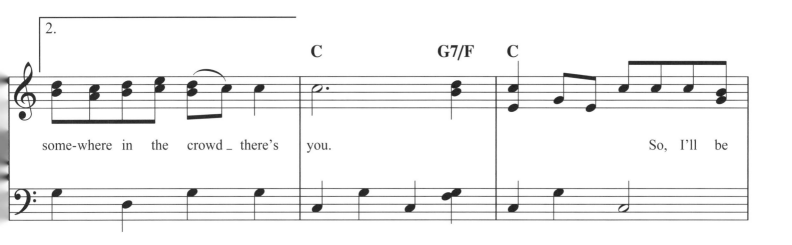

there when you ar - rive, the sight of you will prove to me I'm still a -

live, and when you take me in your arms and hold me tight, I

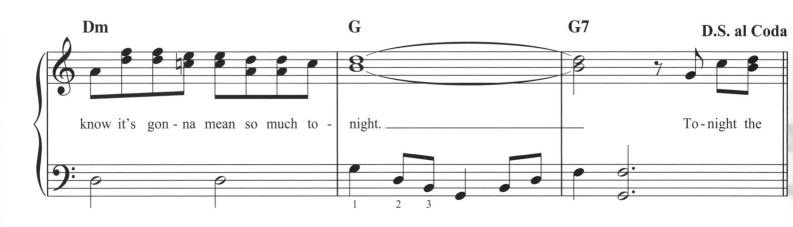

know it's gon - na mean so much to - night. To-night the

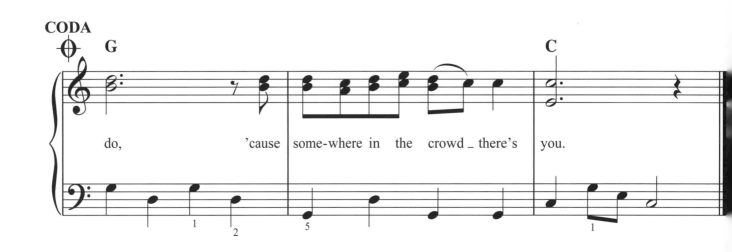

do, 'cause some-where in the crowd _ there's you.

MAYBE IT'S TIME
from A STAR IS BORN

Words and Music by
MICHAEL ISBELL

Moderately slow, in 2

May-be it's time _ to let the old _ ways _ die.

May-be it's time _ to let the old _ ways _ die.

Takes a lot _ to change _ a man, _ hell, it takes a lot _ to try. _

May-be it's time __ to let the old __ ways __ die. __

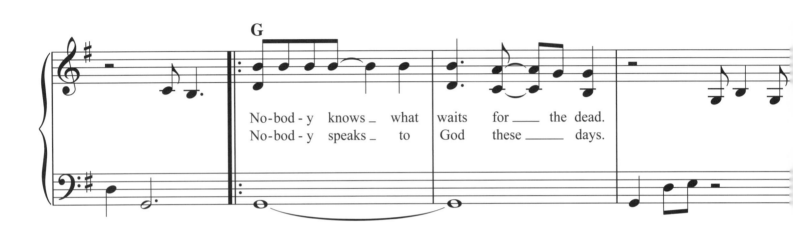

No-bod - y knows __ what waits for __ the dead.
No-bod - y speaks __ to God these _____ days.

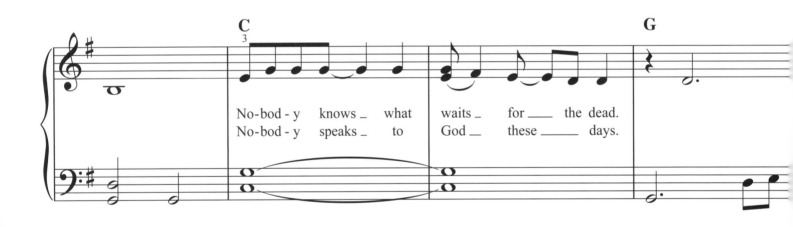

No-bod - y knows __ what waits __ for __ the dead.
No-bod - y speaks __ to God __ these _____ days.

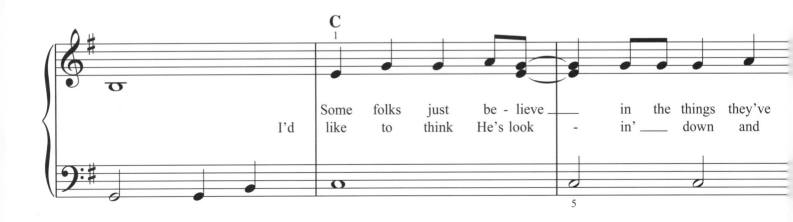

Some folks just be - lieve _____ in the things they've
I'd like to think He's look - in' ____ down and

5

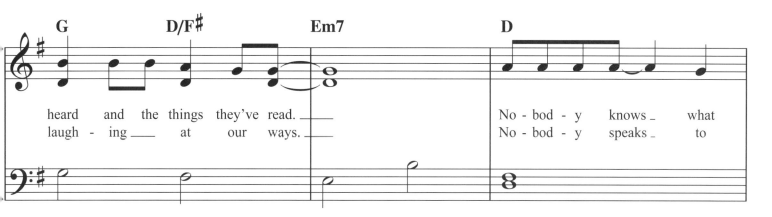

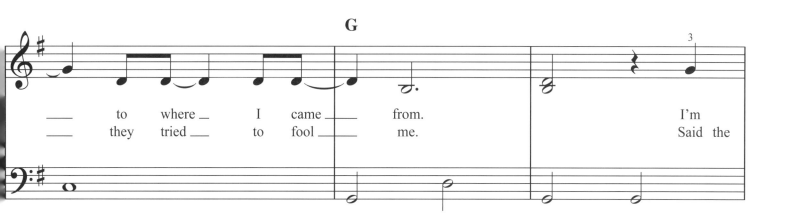

if I could ___ take | spir - its from my | past and bring 'em here,
I've seen hell ___ in | Re - no and | this world's one big

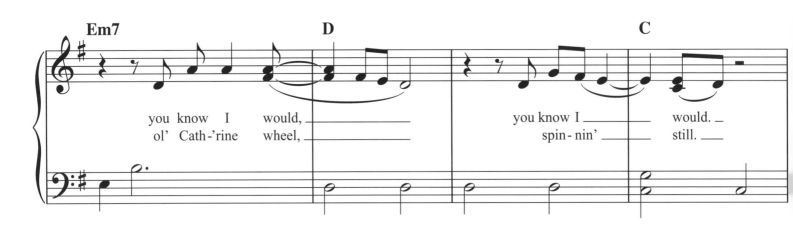

you know I would, ___ | you know I ___ would. __
ol' Cath-'rine wheel, ___ | spin - nin' ___ still. __

May - be it's time __ to let the old ___ ways ___ die.

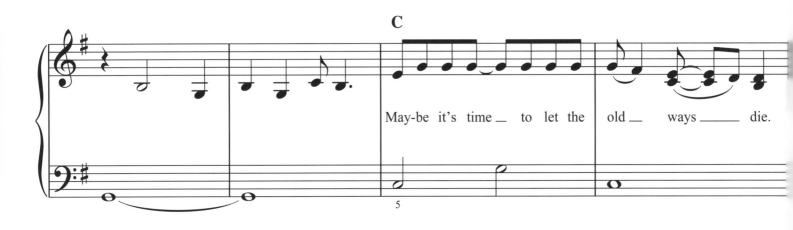

May-be it's time __ to let the old ___ ways ___ die.

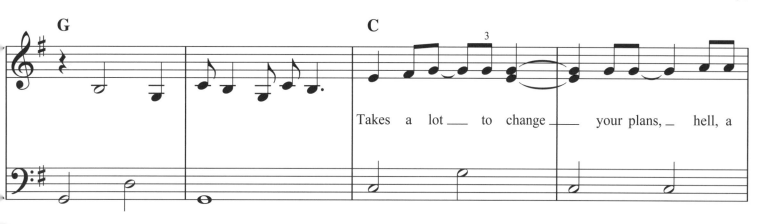

Takes a lot __ to change __ your plans, __ hell, a

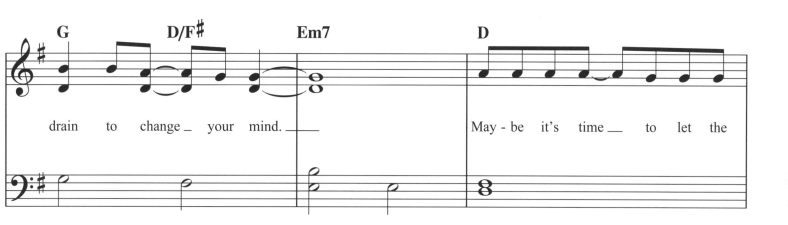

drain to change __ your mind. __ May - be it's time __ to let the

old __ ways __ die. __ Oh, __ may-be it's time __ to let the

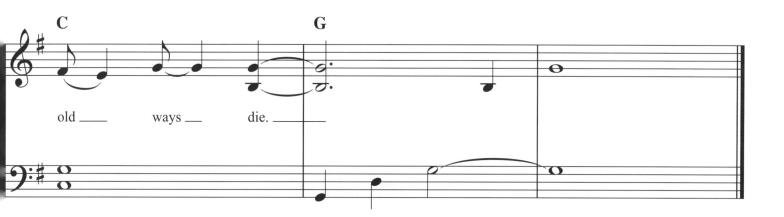

old __ ways __ die. __

ALWAYS REMEMBER US THIS WAY
from A STAR IS BORN

Words and Music by STEFANI GERMANOTTA,
HILLARY LINDSEY, NATALIE HEMBY
and LORI McKENNA

Moderately slow Ballad

That Ar - i - zo - na sky burn-ing in your eyes. ___ You
night, po - ets tryin' to write. ___ We

look at me ___ and, babe, ___ I wan - na catch on fire. ___ It's bur-ied in my
don't know how ___ to rhyme, ___ but damn, we try. ___ But all I real - ly

soul like Cal - i - for - nia gold. ___ You
know: you're where I wan - na go. ___ The

found the light in me ___ that I could-n't find. ___ So, when I'm
part of me ___ that's you ___ will nev - er die. ___

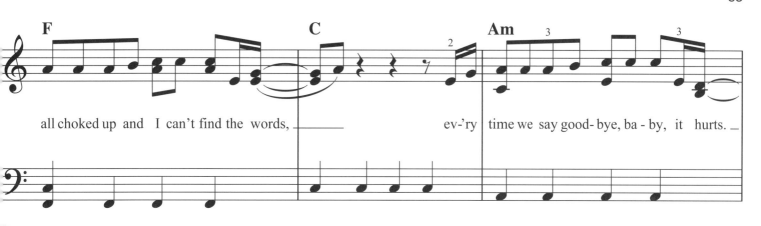

all choked up and I can't find the words, ____ ev-'ry time we say good-bye, ba - by, it hurts. _

_ When the sun goes down _ and the band won't play, _ I'll

al - ways _ re-mem - ber us _ this way. Lov-ers in the way, oh, yeah. _

I don't wan-na be just a mem-o-ry, ba - by, yeah. Ooh, ___ ooh, ___ ooh, ooh.

Ooh, _____ ooh, _____ ooh, ooh. Ooh, _____ ooh, _____ ooh, ooh, ooh.

_____ When I'm all choked up and I can't find _ the words,

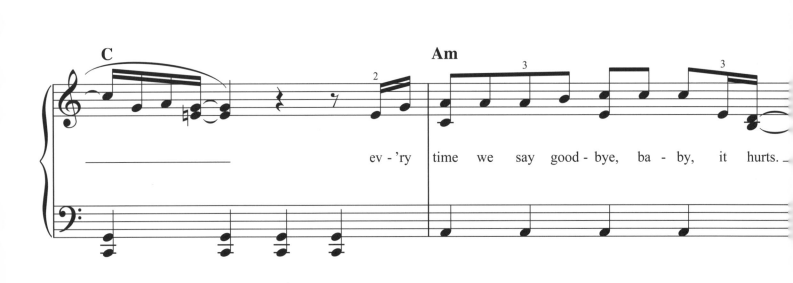

_____ ev-'ry time we say good-bye, ba-by, it hurts. _

_____ When the sun goes down _ and the band won't play, _ I'll

al - ways _ re-mem - ber us _ this way, _ way, _ yeah. _ When you

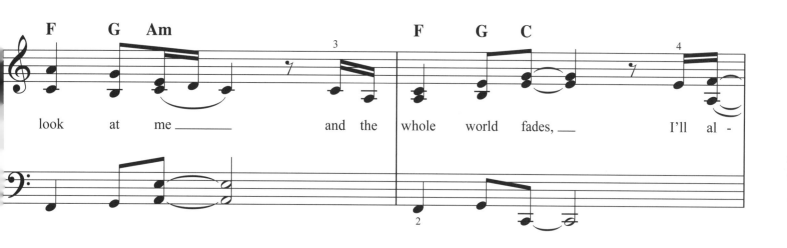

look at me _ and the whole world fades, _ I'll al -

- ways _ re - mem - ber us _ this way. _

Ooh, ooh. _ Oh, _ mm.

I'LL NEVER LOVE AGAIN

from A STAR IS BORN

Words and Music by STEFANI GERMANOTTA,
AARON RAITIERE, HILLARY LINDSEY
and NATALIE HEMBY

knew ____ it would be the last time, ____ I would-'ve broke my heart in

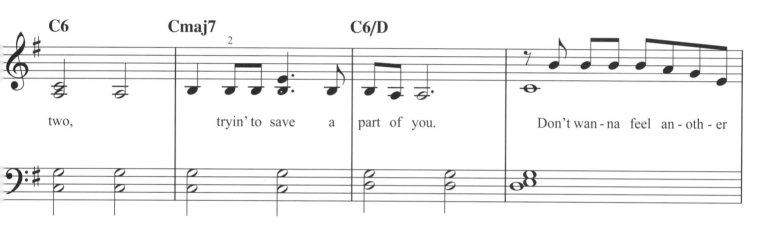

two, tryin' to save a part of you. Don't wan-na feel an-oth-er

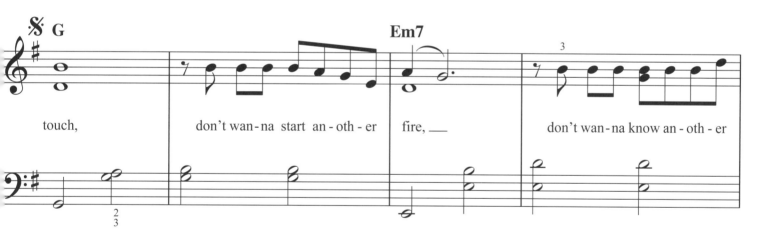

touch, don't wan-na start an-oth-er fire, ___ don't wan-na know an-oth-er

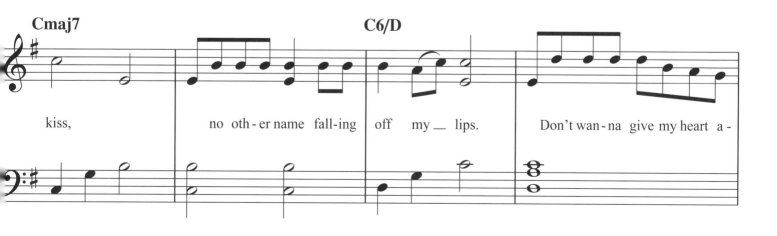

kiss, no oth-er name fall-ing off my __ lips. Don't wan-na give my heart a-

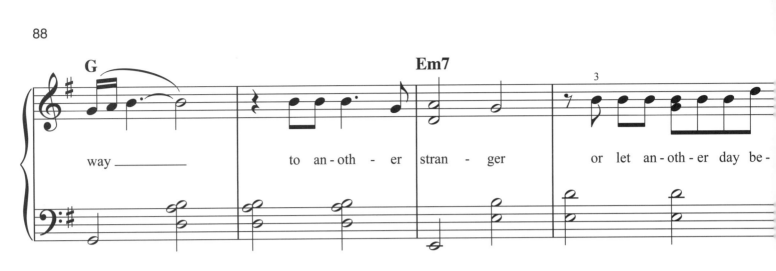

way _____ to an-oth-er stran-ger or let an-oth-er day be-

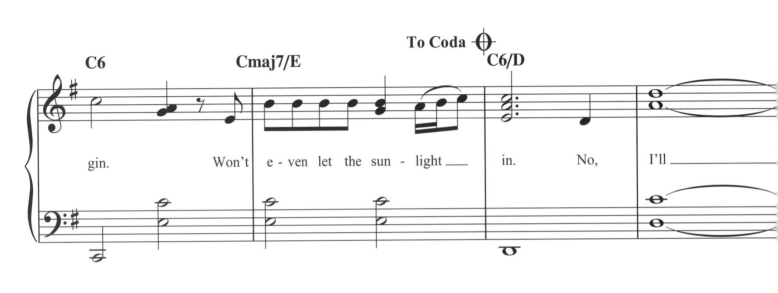

gin. Won't e-ven let the sun-light__ in. No, I'll _____

___ nev-er love a - gain.__ I'll nev-er love a-gain.__

When we first met, I nev-er thought that I would fall. ____

I nev-er thought that I'd find my-self ____ ly-ing in your arms. ____

And I wan-na pre-tend that it's not true, ____ oh, ba-by, let you go. ____

____ 'Cause my world keeps turn-ing and turn-ing and turn-ing, and I'm not

bet - ter part __ of me. _____   I would rath - er wait for you, __   ooh. _____

_____   Don't wan - na feel an - oth - er touch,

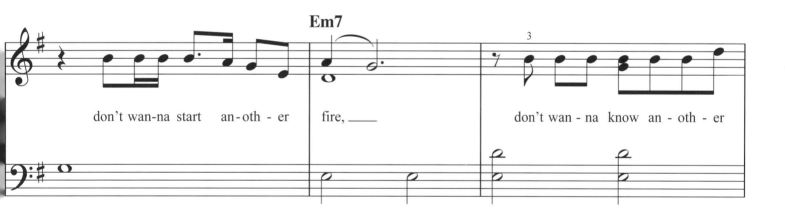

don't wan-na start an-oth - er fire, _____   don't wan - na know an - oth - er

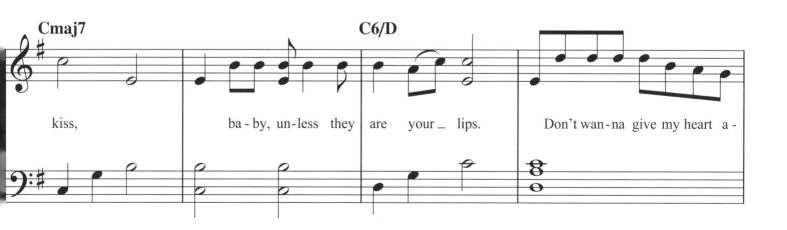

kiss,   ba - by, un-less they are your __ lips.   Don't wan-na give my heart a -

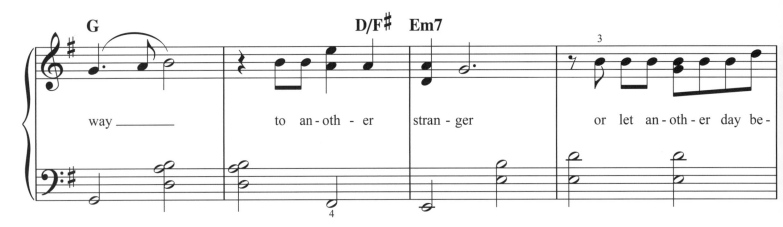

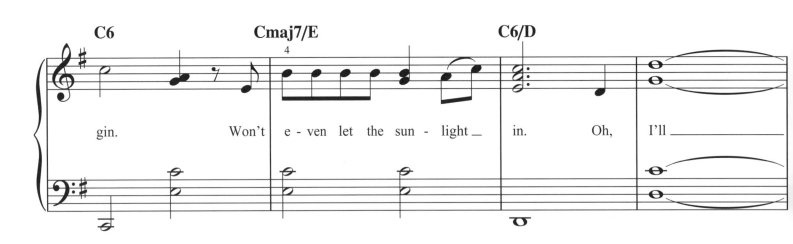

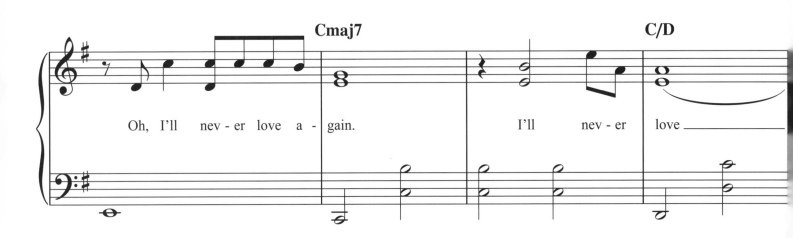

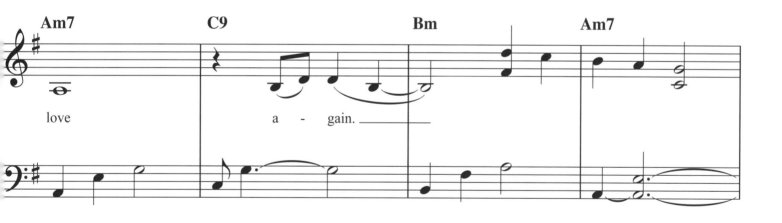

IS THAT ALRIGHT?

from A STAR IS BORN

Words and Music by STEFANI GERMANOTTA,
AARON RAITIERE, NICK MONSON,
LUKAS NELSON, MARK NILAN JR.
and PAUL BLAIR

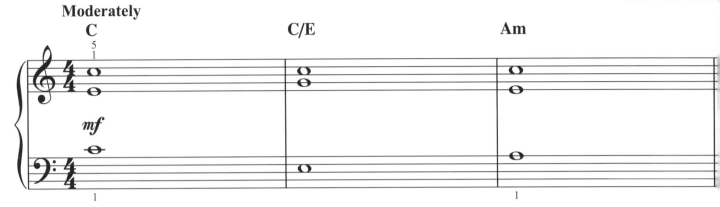

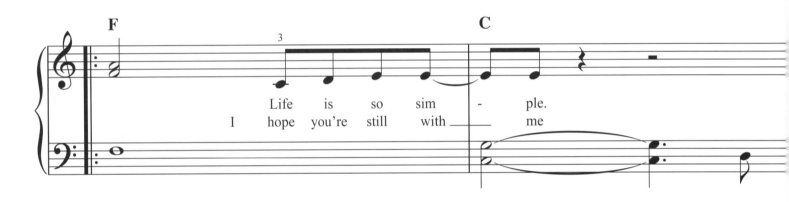

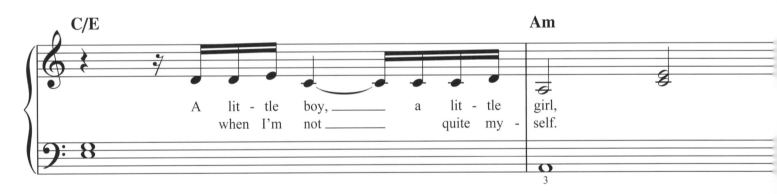

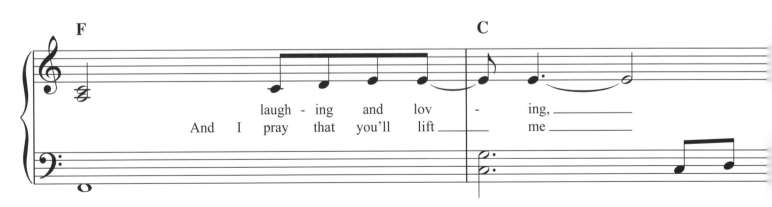

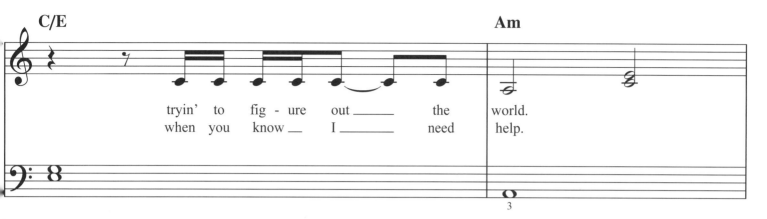

C/E   Am

tryin' to fig - ure out _____ the world.
when you know __ I _____ need help.

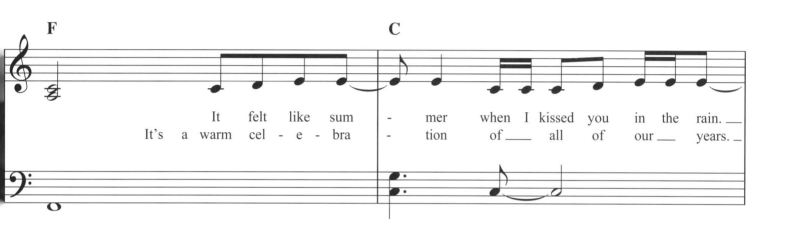

F   C

It felt like sum - mer when I kissed you in the rain. __
It's a warm cel - e - bra - tion of __ all of our __ years. __

C/E   Am   F

__ And I know your sto - ry, but tell me a - gain. __
__ I dream of our sto - ry, of our fair - y tale. __

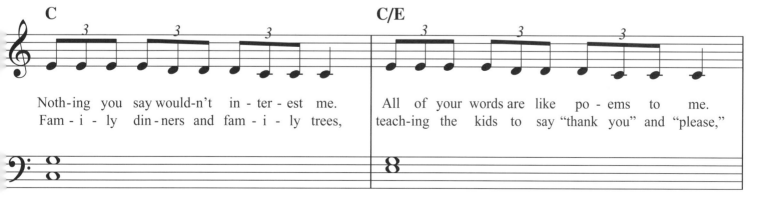

C   C/E

Noth-ing you say would-n't in - ter - est me.
Fam - i - ly din - ners and fam - i - ly trees,

All of your words are like po - ems to me.
teach-ing the kids to say "thank you" and "please,"

at the end of my life. _____ I wan-na see ___ your face ___

_____ when I fall ___ with grace ___ at the mo - ment I die. _____

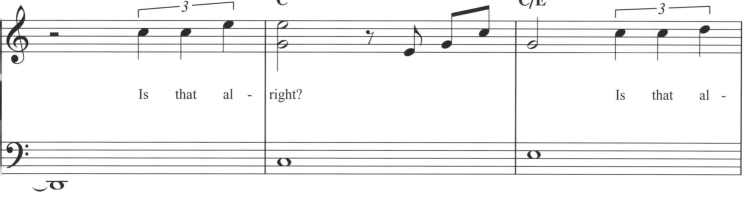

Is that al - right? Is that al -

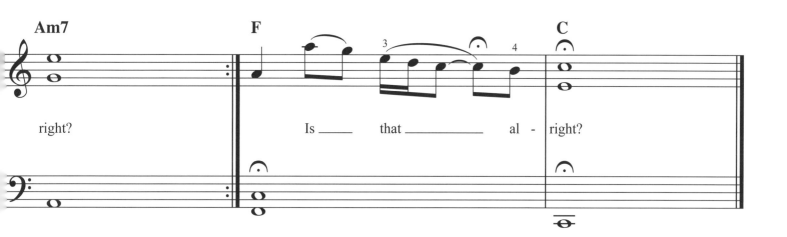

right? Is ___ that _____ al - right?

LOOK WHAT I FOUND

from A STAR IS BORN

Words and Music by STEFANI GERMANOTTA,
AARON RAITIERE, NICK MONSON,
LUKAS NELSON, MARK NILAN JR.
and PAUL BLAIR

back up on my feet, see the lights ___ on ___ the street like stars. ___

___ But look what I found. ___ Look what I ___ found: _

___ an - oth - er piece of my heart ___

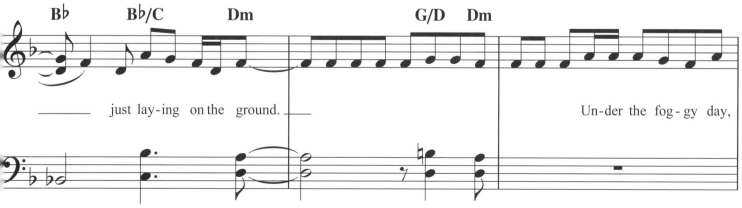

___ just lay-ing on the ground. ___ Un-der the fog-gy day,

100

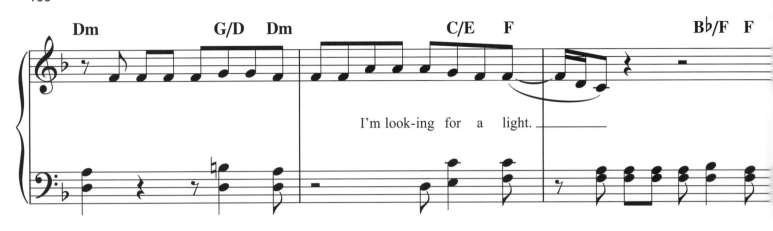

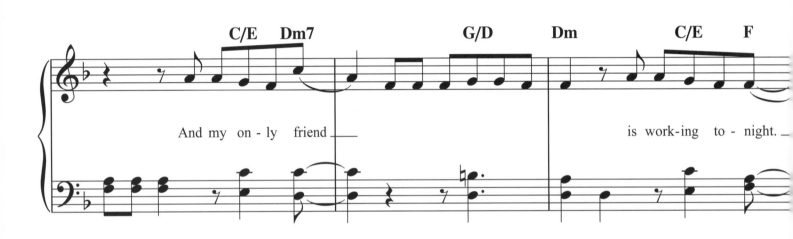

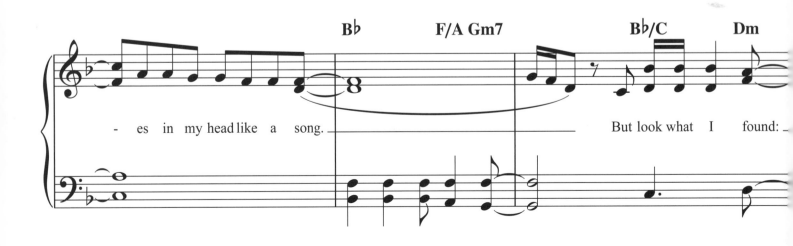

some - bod - y who loves _____ me. Look what I _____ found: _

_____ some - bod - y who'll car - ry 'round a piece of my heart _

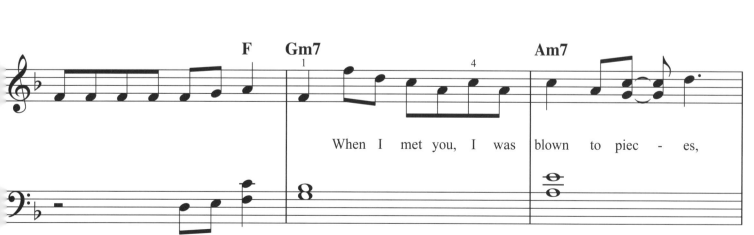

just lay - ing on the ground. _____

When I met you, I was blown to piec - es,

102

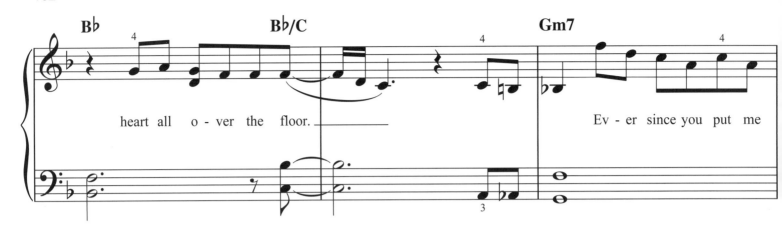

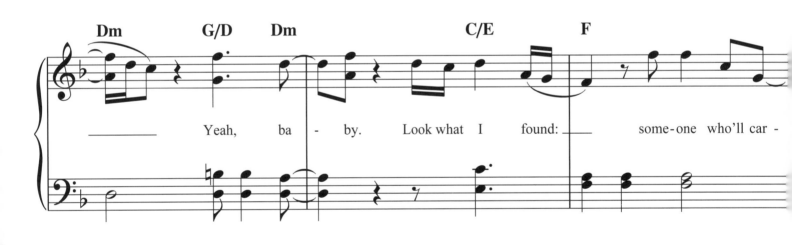

MUSIC TO MY EYES

from A STAR IS BORN

Words and Music by STEFANI GERMANOTTA
and LUKAS NELSON

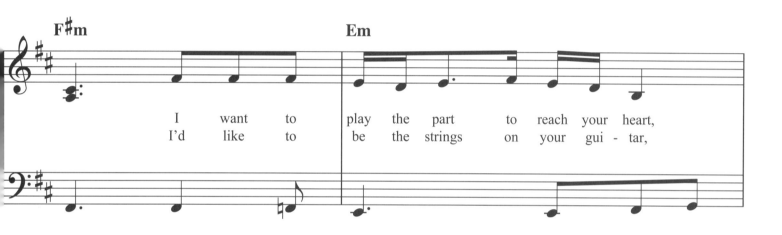

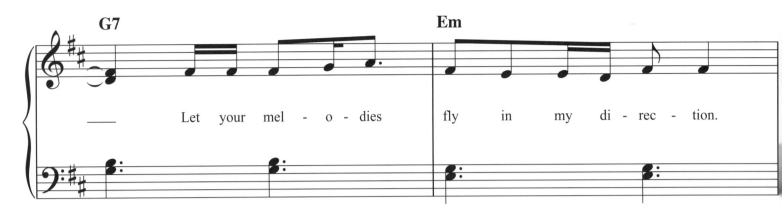

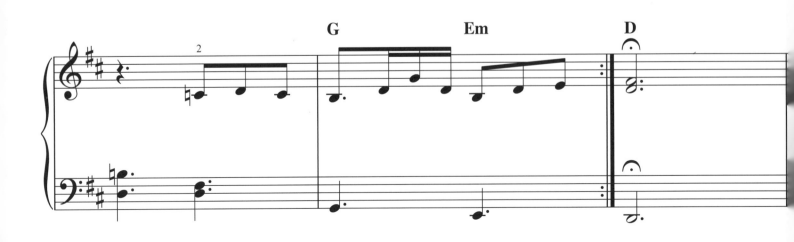

SHALLOW
from A STAR IS BORN

Words and Music by STEFANI GERMANOTTA,
MARK RONSON, ANDREW WYATT
and ANTHONY ROSSOMANDO

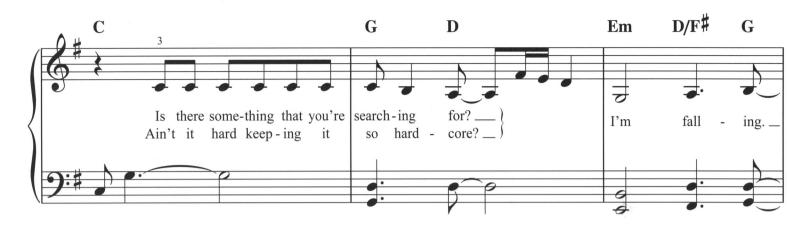

Is there some-thing that you're search-ing for? ___
Ain't it hard keep-ing it so hard-core? ___
I'm fall - ing. ___

___ In all the good times I find my-self ___ long-ing ___

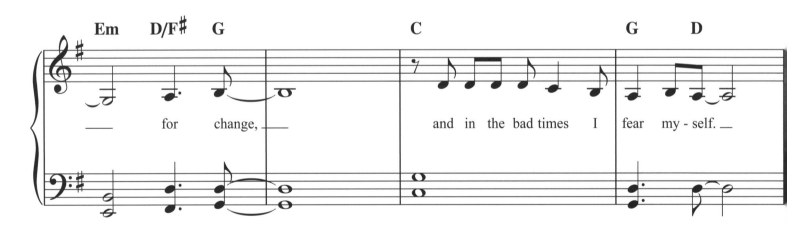

___ for change, ___ and in the bad times I fear my-self. ___

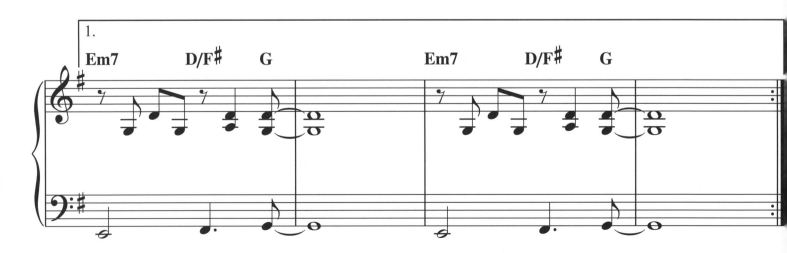

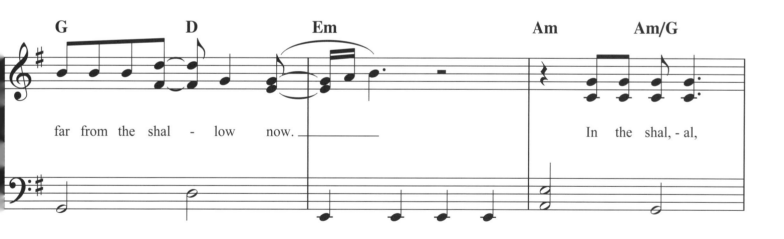

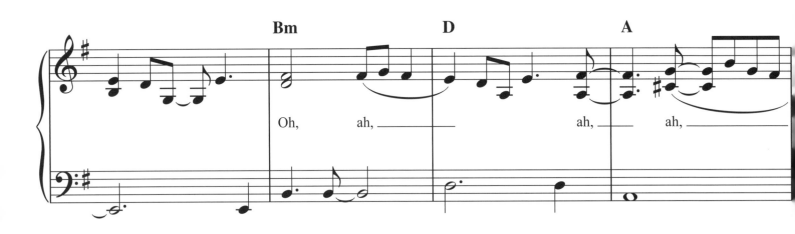

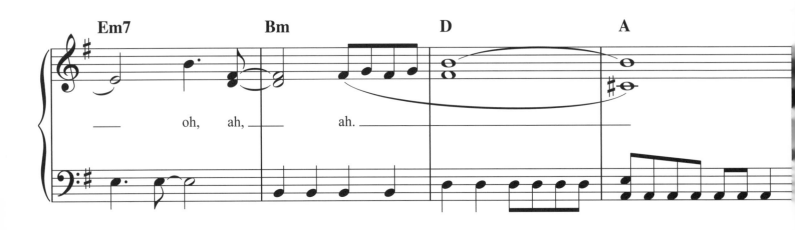

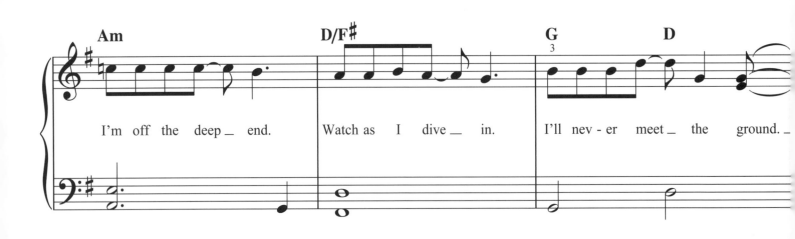

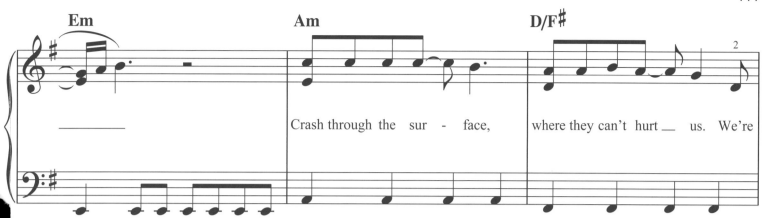

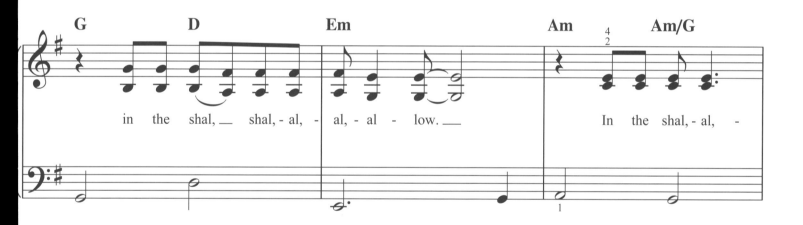

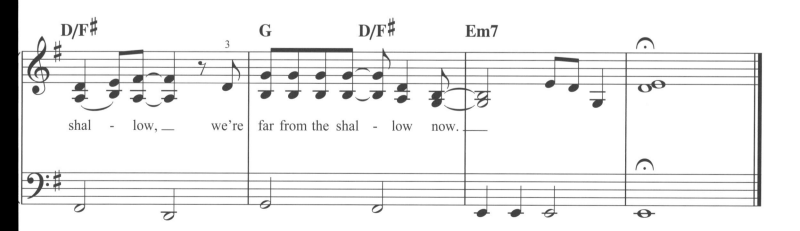

It's Easy to Play Your Favorite Songs with Hal Leonard Easy Piano Books

The Beatles Best – 2nd Edition

120 arrangements for easy piano, including: All My Loving • Dear Prudence • Eleanor Rigby • Good Day Sunshine • In My Life • Let It Be • Michelle • Ob-La-Di, Ob-La-Da • Revolution • Something • Yesterday • and more.
00231944 .... $24.99

The Best Broadway Songs Ever

This bestseller features 80+ Broadway faves: All I Ask of You • I Wanna Be a Producer • Just in Time • My Funny Valentine • On My Own • Seasons of Love • The Sound of Music • Tomorrow • Younger Than Springtime • more!
00300178 .... $22.99

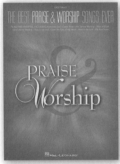

The Best Praise & Worship Songs Ever

The name says it all: over 70 of the best P&W songs today. Titles include: Awesome God • Blessed Be Your Name • Come, Now Is the Time to Worship • Days of Elijah • Here I Am to Worship • Open the Eyes of My Heart • Shout to the Lord • We Fall Down • and more.
00311312 .... $19.99

The Best Songs Ever

Over 70 all-time favorite songs, including: All I Ask of You • Body and Soul • Call Me Irresponsible • Edelweiss • Fly Me to the Moon • The Girl from Ipanema • Here's That Rainy Day • Imagine • Let It Be • Moonlight in Vermont • People • Somewhere Out There • Tears in Heaven • Unforgettable • The Way We Were • and more.
00359223 .... $19.95

Get complete song lists and more at
www.halleonard.com

Prices, contents, and availability subject to change without notice
Disney characters and artwork © Disney Enterprises, Inc.

First 50 Popular Songs You Should Play on the Piano

50 great pop classics for beginning pianists to learn, including: Candle in the Wind • Chopsticks • Don't Know Why • Hallelujah • Happy Birthday to You • Heart and Soul • I Walk the Line • Just the Way You Are • Let It Be • Let It Go • Over the Rainbow • Piano Man • and many more.
00131140 .... $16.99

Jumbo Easy Piano Songbook

200 classical favorites, folk songs and jazz standards. Includes: Amazing Grace • Beale Street Blues • Bridal Chorus • Buffalo Gals • Canon in D • Cielito Lindo • Danny Boy • The Entertainer • Für Elise • Greensleeves • Jamaica Farewell • Marianne • Molly Malone • Ode to Joy • Peg O' My Heart • Rockin' Robin • Yankee Doodle • dozens more!
00311014 .... $19.99

Best Children's Songs Ever – 2nd Edition

This amazing collection features 101 songs, including: Beauty and the Beast • Do-Re-Mi • Hakuna Matata • Happy Birthday to You • If I Only Had a Brain • Let It Go • On Top of Spaghetti • Over the Rainbow • Puff the Magic Dragon • Rubber Duckie • Winnie the Pooh • and many more.
00159272 .... $19.99

150 of the Most Beautiful Songs Ever

Easy arrangements of 150 of the most popular songs of our time. Includes: Bewitched • Fly Me to the Moon • How Deep Is Your Love • My Funny Valentine • Some Enchanted Evening • Tears in Heaven • Till There Was You • Yesterday • You Are So Beautiful • and more. 550 pages of great music!
00311316 .... $24.95

50 Easy Classical Themes

Easy arrangements of 50 classical tunes representing more than 30 composers, including: Bach, Beethoven, Chopin, Debussy, Dvorak, Handel, Haydn, Liszt, Mozart, Mussorgsky, Puccini, Rossini, Schubert, Strauss, Tchaikovsky, Vivaldi, and more.
00311215 .... $14.99

Popular Sheet Music – 30 Hits from 2015-2017

30 songs: Burn • Cheap Thrills • City of Stars • Don't Wanna Know • HandClap • H.O.L.Y. • Love on the Weekend • Million Reasons • Ophelia • Ride • Say You Won't Let Go • 7 Years • Shape of You • This Town • When We Were Young • and more.
00233043 .... $17.99

VH1's 100 Greatest Songs of Rock and Roll

The results from the VH1 show that featured the 100 greatest rock and roll songs of all time are here in this awesome collection! Songs include: Born to Run • Good Vibrations • Hey Jude • Hotel California • Imagine • Light My Fire • Like a Rolling Stone • Respect • and more.
00311110 .... $29.99

Disney's My First Song Book

16 favorite songs to sing and play. Every page is beautifully illustrated with full-color art from Disney features. Songs include: Beauty and the Beast • Bibbidi-Bobbidi-Boo • Circle of Life • Cruella De Vil • A Dream Is a Wish Your Heart Makes • Hakuna Matata • Under the Sea • Winnie the Pooh • You've Got a Friend in Me • and more.
00310322 .... $16.99

HAL•LEONARD